PURPOSE DRIVEN FAMILY

PURPOSE
Driven Family

Dr. Chibundo Marchie

PURPOSE DRIVEN FAMILY

REHOBOTH HOUSETM

Copyright © 2020 by Dr. Chibundo Marchie

Purpose Driven Family

ISBN: 978-1-64301-020-5

Unless otherwise indicated, all scripture quotations are taken from the Authorized King James Version of the Holy Bible (KJV).

The opinions expressed by the author in this book are exclusively hers and not of Rehoboth House. Contact Dr. Chibundo for counseling, teachings, seminars, and workshops.

Book Available Online
www.amazon.com
www.barnesandnoble.com
www.gimfglobal.org
Other Major Online Bookstores

Contact For Enquiries
Call: 804-502-1926
Email:chibundoanene@yahoo.com

Author's Contact
Email: chibundoanene@yahoo.com

Published By Rehoboth House, Chicago
Email: info@rehobothhouseonline.com
www. rehobothhouseonline.com

Cover And Interior Design
Rehoboth House, Chicago

Printed in the United States of America, April 2020

REHOBOTH HOUSE

PURPOSE DRIVEN FAMILY

TABLE OF CONTENTS

NOTE:

In other to enhance readability and comprehension, the author adopted the acronym - PDF for Purpose Driven Family.

CHAPTER 1

Commitment & Focus In Purpose Driven Family

This theme is so dear to my heart, it is a series that has blessed my family tremendously, and I am putting it in a book, believing it will bless you and your family as well; taking you to God's ultimate plan.

From the beginning, God has been interested in the family. A family is a dynamic unit for accomplishing His will. The family is made up of individuals connected by blood and knitted in love. The love and bond that exists in the family are so strong that when the members set their minds on a purpose, nothing can stop them. This is why God is interested in committing His purpose to a family; likewise, the devil is interested in families too but of course, for a very different reason.

The first people God created were family, Adam and Eve, then Cain and Abel. God told Abraham that through Him all the families will be blessed. God has the family in mind, even your family. He has plans of blessing families. God lost the first family in Adam but now has redeemed families back to Himself by the blood of Jesus. That means every member of your family can be saved and united to achieve God's purpose and vision.

> *"Now the Lord had said unto Abram, Get thee out of thy country, and from thy kindred, and from thy father's house, unto a land that I will shew thee: And I will make of thee a great nation, and I will bless thee, and make thy name great; and thou shalt be a blessing: And I will bless them that bless thee, and curse him that curseth thee: and in thee shall all families of the earth be blessed" (Gen.12:1-3).*

Before I go on, I would like to define Purpose Driven Family (PDF) as a family whose members are motivated by one purpose, pulling their resources, gifts, and talents together to achieve a particular purpose. In the context of this book, this purpose is God's purpose; vision.

At creation, God gave the first family a purpose (Genesis 1:26-31). And no sooner did they set to achieve it; the devil deceived them from the purpose. That is why today, many families are driven by purposes other than God's. Families are driven by their purpose; traditional purpose, political, satanic, father, mother, society purposes, and so on.

I tell you, any purpose other than God's is detrimental to the family and under maximizes her potential. Until your family is motivated and living by God's purpose, the individual members will not maximize their potential and realize all the blessing God has for them. When you pursue God's purpose, you will obtain all the blessings God has in store for you as a family. The talent that God has placed in every family member is for His purpose.

A good example of a purpose driven family (PDF) is Noah's family. Noah is a good example of a family that realized God's purpose in a world filled with distractions just like ours today.

Noah and his family were totally committed and focused. They were not distracted. Every member of the family was on board; contributing their various abilities. God's purpose is something every member should be involved with.

"The body growth by what every joint supplieth" (Eph. 4:16).

I shall consider Noah's family under these headings to bless your life and family.

- God's Purpose For Noah's Family?

- Noah's Leadership Example

- Their Society And Limitations

- Their Commitment

- And Their Reward

God's Purpose For Noah's Family? Genesis 6:11-24

God commanded Noah and his family to build an ark. Noah was living at a time when people were evil and corrupt, but God chose him to build an ark to redeem his generation. The ark is a symbol of Salvation. For God so loved the world, that he gave his only begotten Son, that whosoever believeth in him should not perish, but have everlasting life. (John 3:16). The gospel of Jesus is for Salvation and Redemption of all.

Just like God committed the building of the ark to Noah, He has committed the gospel of Jesus to every family. God wants every family to be committed to the preaching of the gospel; to be part of the gospel work, using your talents, resources, and abilities to spread the gospel. You and your family are positioned where you are because of the gospel.

As you get involved in the gospel business, it will not only save you, it will also save others. Identify a gospel movement and be involved with it. Do not be a visitor in your local church or ministry. Be involved in the gospel business. This can only be done through commitment.

People in Noah's day were dinning, winning, getting married and giving to marriage (Matthew 24:38) but he and his family were focused on building the ark. They were committed; despite numerous distractions. This is exactly like today's world, where people are engaged in various activities, no one has time for the gospel, but you and your family must succeed as gospel propellers.

You must be focused, committed, and not be entangled with the affairs of this life. You are sent to where you are because of the corruption of the people, so keep yourselves focused on the commission, unspotted, to impact those around you. You cannot live anyhow and be drowned with the people you are sent to save. Do not imitate their worldly ways.

God expects other families to be blessed by your commitment to His purpose. As you get committed to the gospel business, people that come to you will be pointed to the ark for their salvation. So be committed in such a way to influence people unto salvation.

> *"I beseech you, therefore, brethren, by the mercies of God, that ye present your bodies a living sacrifice, holy, acceptable unto God, which is your reasonable service. And be not conformed to this world: but be ye transformed by the renewing of your mind, that ye may prove what is that good, and acceptable, and perfect, will of God" (Rom.12:1-2).*

> *"And I brought your fathers out of Egypt: and ye came unto the sea, and the Egyptians pursued after your fathers with chariots and horsemen unto the Red sea" (Joshua 24:6).*

Your prayer as a family should be "Lord, help us to realize your purpose so that we may lead others to you. Keep us from the ways of the people. In this dark world, we shall walk in your light unto our destiny. We are family on course with destiny, even to all generation. Help us to be like Jesus. Amen"

Noah's Leadership Example

Noah was a man of obedience and faith worthy of emulation.

> *"Thus did Noah; according to all that God commanded him, so did he" (Gen.6:22).*

> *"By faith Noah, being warned of God of things not seen as yet, moved with fear, prepared an ark to the saving of his house; by the which he condemned the world, and became heir of the righteousness which is by faith" (Heb.11:7).*

During Noah's time, it has never rained, and the people didn't even know what rain was, but when God warned him about the rain, he believed and obeyed, not minding what people might say. By faith, through obedience, he embarked on the new walk with God. It takes faith to walk with God into the unknown.

God's purpose for your family might be uncommon, would you, like Noah risk it all by Faith despite your fears and what people might say? Do you believe God enough to depend on His word for your entire life, putting your life on the line? Can you as family heed to God's warning or do you neglect His counsel?

Noah feared God and obeyed what He said. Do you take everything else in your life important but His word? When it comes to God do you have this attitude of 'anything can go,' 'God understands.' These are wrong attitudes. You have to acknowledge as a family that your entire life depends on what He says and what you have to do.

Noah was a good leader, he got everyone on board. Not even one of his family members was left out. No price is too much to pay to win every member of your family to Christ and His purpose. Therefore, sell God's purpose in a way that everyone sees the benefit to be committed. No one is too big for God's purpose. If you love your family and care about them, you should be concerned about their salvation. Your joy is incomplete without the salvation of all the members of your family.

Rahab got every member of her family on board (Joshua 2). Jesus' earthly family was involved in the gospel business. Abraham commanded his household to walk in God's ways (Gen.18:18-19). Teach your children in the way they should go (Deut.6). Lot lost his wife. Get every member on board because you all have different gifts and talent required for the work. Serve God in such a way to provoke them to join.

> *"Wherefore say, Behold, I give unto him my covenant of peace: And he shall have it, and his seed after him, even the covenant of an everlasting priesthood; because he was zealous for his God, and made an atonement for the children of Israel" (Num. 25:12-13).*

Noah was a patient man. He built the ark for one hundred and twenty years. He did not give up even when there was no sign of rain. He was devoted and generous towards God's purpose to the end.

Their Reward

God's purpose comes to prevent catastrophe in your life if obeyed. When the whole earth was destroyed only Noah, and his family was preserved. Arise, shine; for thy light is come, and the glory of the LORD is risen upon thee. For, behold, the darkness shall cover the earth, and gross darkness the people: but the LORD shall arise upon thee, and his glory shall be seen upon thee." (Isaiah 60:1-2)

God's purpose is your escape route out of destruction. Noah's family was saved from the flood by God's purpose. When others were drowning, they were lifted. God's purpose is for your Distinction, Preservation and Honour. If you care to be different by God's purpose, you will be distinguished and preserved.

God's purpose through David exempted his family from tax and tribute in Israel. God's purpose established God's covenant with you, making God responsible for you. When your family is fulfilling God's purpose, heaven supports you and God takes over your needs. (Malachi 3:14-4:3, Ex. 23:23-27). These are just a few of the numerous benefits.

In a purpose driven family (PDF), only one thing matters; that is God's purpose and Kingdom business. PDF should be willing to sacrifice anything to achieve God's purpose. Your family is here on a mission, do not be distracted. God depends on you to accomplish His purpose.

CHAPTER 2

Leadership In Purpose Driven Family

This chapter is very important because without a leader the family is without direction and is going nowhere. Everyone will do what he or she pleases. It takes a leader for a family to accomplish God's purpose. The question is, who is the leader in the purpose driven family? In other words, who does God depend on to get the family to accomplish His purpose? Every family is created by God, and God is the ultimate head. He determines the purpose for every family and therefore depends on anyone that will lay hold on His purpose to lead the family towards the same purpose.

"We know that in all things God works for good with those who love him, those whom he has called according to his purpose" (Romans 8:28).

God is the leader in the purpose driven family (PDF) but needs a person; a physical body he can pass His directions through. He inhabits the person by His Spirit and leads through him. For the Israelites, God was their leader, but He led them by Moses. As Moses spent time with God, he got specific instructions and word and then relayed it to the Israelites. God made his ways and acts known unto Moses and through him to the Israelites. When God appeared and spoke to them, they were so terrified by his voice and presence, and they asked him to lead them through Moses.

What am I saying? A leader in purpose driven family interprets and simplifies the vision for everyone to understand. This is leadership; understanding God's purpose and conveying it for others to understand and follow.

Habakkuk 2:1-3 describes the process of leadership:

1) Waiting on God

2) Getting the purpose (word)

3) Relaying the purpose

4) Getting people committed.

> *"I will stand upon my watch, and set me upon the tower, and will watch to see what he will say unto me, and what I shall answer when I am reproved. And the LORD answered me, and said, Write the vision, and make it plain upon tables, that he may run that readeth it. For the vision is yet for an appointed time, but at the end, it shall speak, and not lie: though it tarry, wait for it; because it will surely come, it will not tarry" (Habakkuk 2:1-3).*

God works through men that will yield their spirit, soul, and body to Him to lead others. The spirit, soul, and body come to play for effective leadership; yielding the spirit, soul, and body for God to inspire and energize others.

Renew your soul (mind, will, emotion, intellect, and thoughts) to interpret and believe God's leading. Do not be distracted by the sensual inputs, but be strong. The body should be strong and fit to relay and run with God's purpose.

Leadership in PDF is to provide direction towards fulfilling God's purpose, and not man's purpose, political purpose or societal purpose, etc. The leader in PDF should steer the family unto God's purpose. Abraham is a very good PDF leader.

> *"Seeing that Abraham shall surely become a great and mighty nation, and all the nations of the earth shall be blessed in him? For I know him, that he will command his children and his household after him, and they shall keep the way of the LORD, to do justice and judgment; that the LORD may bring upon Abraham that which he hath spoken of him" (Gen 18:18-19).*

In every family, the father by his position is expected to be the leader, assisted by the mother. But in God's purpose driven family God is not bound by that; for He is not a respecter of persons *(Romans 2:11),* but every member who seeks Him and His will is acceptable by him. When God finds a family member that seeks him and His purpose, He entrusts the leadership of the entire family to him or her.

> *"Better is a poor and a wise child than an old and foolish king, who will no more be admonished" (Eccl 4:13).*

> *"For to him that is joined to all the living there is hope: for a living dog is better than a dead lion" (Eccl 9:4).*

The Lion is the king of the forest, but what good is a dead Lion. A dog that is alive is better than a lion that is dead. So when the lion is dead, a dog that is alive, though of less strength takes over leadership. In the same way, no man whether man or woman can lead a family into God's purpose when he is spiritually dead and insensitive to God's will and ways. Eternally, God cannot lead through the spiritually dead.

The men of Issachar knew and understood the times, what Israel was supposed to be doing and were in command. Although they were not the first tribe, they became leaders by insight. Being the first child in a family does not automatically make you the leader in God's purpose, what makes you a leader is your understanding of what needs to be done per time.

> *"And of the children of Issachar, which were men that had understanding of the times, to know what Israel ought to do; the heads of them were two hundred; and all their brethren were at their commandment." (I Chron12:32)*

Zachariah lost leadership to his wife, Elizabeth at the birth of John the Baptist. He was dumb and could not speak therefore lost his leadership position. You lead by your voice, as you speak God's will. When your voice, what you say contradicts what God is doing or wants to do, be careful, or you will lose your leadership position. The essence of parenting it to stir the family unto God's purpose.

> *"Yet ye say, Wherefore? Because the LORD hath been witness between thee and the wife of thy youth, against whom thou hast dealt treacherously: yet is she thy companion, and the wife of thy covenant. And did not he make one? Yet had he the residue of the spirit. And wherefore one? That he might seek a godly seed. Therefore take heed to your spirit, and let none deal treacherously against the wife of his youth" (Malachi 2:14-15).*

Will God stand and watch the family he has redeemed with his blood not led a right person? What need is a father or mother who does not lead his or her children in the fear and admonition of God; cultivating their potential to fulfill God's purpose? Children are God's heritage, God's own not any man's. But how can a father or mother lead, if he or she spends hours on TV rather than waiting on God?

History has it that Smith Wigglesworth a man greatly used by God. He never allowed even the dailies into his house; only the Bible and godly materials were read in his house. That was a purpose driven family. When a father or mother that should be the leader spends the most time on films, he or she is feeding the mind with trash, and in turn leads the family into trash, disgrace, and shame. His or her mind is filled with trash, far from God's will. Tell me how on earth would such a person be effective in that divine position? God's position is not in titles but in function. What makes you relevant in that position is the divine function you perform!

I wake up early to get specific instruction from God and remain relevant as a mother and leader in the ministry; otherwise, someone else will take my place. This is the secret of the virtuous woman. She wakes early and provides everyone with the relevant meat of God's word.

> *"She riseth also while it is yet night, and giveth meat to her household, and a portion to her maidens."(Prov. 31:15)*

God does not respect anyone. He honours you to the extent you know and do what He expects you to do. And when you are relevant and win His respect, people will give you the honour you deserve. Do not seek for honour, seek to please God. Remain relevant, and you will be respected and honoured.

As a leader, renew your mind with God's word and discern what God is doing in your family, otherwise you will constitute a nuisance to the people you are supposed to lead.

"Woe to thee, O land, when thy king is a child, and thy princes eat in the morning!" (Eccl.10:16).

"The rich man is wise in his own conceit, but the poor that hath understanding searcheth him out. When righteous men do rejoice, there is great glory: but when the wicked rise, a man is hidden" (Prov. 28:10-11).

When the supposed leader is a child; unskilful in the word of God, the family is cursed; empowered to fail. The word of God is what matures and establishes you in a leadership position. "All scripture is given by inspiration of God, and is profitable for doctrine, for reproof, for correction, for instruction in righteousness: That the man of God may be perfect, thoroughly furnished unto all good works" (2 Tim. 3:16-17).

Do not let your schedule deter you from the word making you irrelevant in your divine position and assignment. Above every other role you play in your family, you are a leader in God's purpose. You are what you spend the most time on. What you do most is what you think about most. And what you think about most is who you are. If most of your time is not spent on God's word and prayer, you are not qualified for leadership in the purpose driven family. *"Can two walk together except they be agreed?" (Amos 3:3).* If you do not spend time on the word and prayers, you cannot walk with God nor lead others in his purpose. Your mind has to be constantly renewed to keep trend with God.

Moses lost leadership to Joshua; he was not renewed to the new style of leadership. Rather than talk to the Rock as instructed by God, he struck it. As a mother or father in a purpose driven family, no one is contending your leadership position, only remain relevant by daily renewing of your mind by the word, or you will be confusing people. You cannot just read a few verses of the scriptures or devotional as a parent and want to successfully lead your family. The light of God's word you have must shine brighter than those of the people you are leading; so much as to gain their attention. This is automatic leadership. When your light shines brightly, people will by themselves come to you, and this is leadership.

"And the Gentiles shall come to thy light, and kings to the brightness of thy rising" (Isaiah 60:3).

You do not need to coerce, manipulate, intimidate or force people. Leadership is designed to be spontaneous. If you refuse to labour in the word, you will struggle to lead men. Pursue God by your studying of the word and men will pursue and submit to you. During your family altar, share revelation from God's word to empower everyone, and not same old stuff all the time. Wait on God and get fresh revelation for your family needs to be empowered and moved forward. As a leader, you do not only study for yourself but for others also.

"All scripture is given by inspiration of God, and is profitable for doctrine, for reproof, for correction, for instruction in

righteousness: That the man of God may be perfect, thoroughly furnished unto all good works" (2Tim.3:16-17).

The Bible is given for effective leadership. Eli lost leadership to Samuel. Watch it, that boy might soon take over. If you don't know, people are waiting to take your place. Otherwise, God would not say hold fast that which you have so that no one takes it from you.

"Behold, I come quickly: hold that fast which thou hast, that no man take thy crown" (Revelation 3:11).

Be relevant, those kids are looking up to you for fresh revelation from the word. To the glory of God, my family altar is very exciting, and everyone is eager to take notes.

I cannot afford to be slack least any man take my place. There is no complacency in leadership. Leadership is not by title, it is earned through functionality. Be disciplined on the word of God. There is so much the word does to make you an able leader. It infuses you with the life of God, the greatest leader.

Everything you need to be an effective leader is impacted by the word. You may even be the last in the family as David, unheard of and forgotten, only lay hold on the word and you will come out of every "following of ewes" to leading people. You are coming out of every obscurity, and your voice will be heard. Just stick to the word, for no one lights a candle and covers it up.

> *"No man, when he hath lighted a candle, covereth it with a vessel, or putteth it under a bed; but setteth it on a candlestick, that they which enter in may see the light" (Luke 8:16).*

Leadership position is open to whosoever pays the price, running in such a way to be in front, for others to follow. Do not let anyone despise your youth, you can lead. God is no respecter of person *(Romans 2:11)*. Though you might be under good leadership, God expects you to access the light for your path.

Timothy though under godly leadership of his mother and grandmother knew the word for himself. As a father or mother, you owe it to your family to study the word; renewing your mind with what God is doing and lead them rightly. It is your responsibility to your family. You cannot lead when your mind is unrenewed and far from God.

> *"And be not conformed to this world: but be ye transformed by the renewing of your mind, that ye may prove what is that good, and acceptable, and perfect, will of God" (Romans 12:2).*

As a leader your word time should not be compromised, rather it should surpass that of the people you lead. People should be confident to find God's will from you. That's what leadership is for, to proffer direction. Only the word will make you an effective leader; not tradition, religion or custom. Until your spirit is lightened with the word, you cannot be placed on the table to give light to everyone that comes into the room.

"Neither do men light a candle, and put it under a bushel, but on a candlestick; and it giveth light unto all that are in the house" (Matthew 5:15).

My father was a very good leader of my family, not because of money, strength or status, but in knowing God's will. His word time is the most consistent I have ever known. He spends not less than three hours daily on the word. And his mind was so renewed that no one doubts him when it comes to knowing God's will. His counsel is conclusive and divine. When Papa says it, you do not need to pray further. We have seen the things he said come to pass. Papa did not have all the money to throw on us, but we appreciated and treasured his godly leadership.

"Train up a child in the way he should go: and when he is old, he will not depart from it" (Proverbs 22:6).

What makes you an effective leader in the purpose driven family is not the money you throw around or the houses you built but people's confident assurance in your godly counsel. Be sincere and bold in leading your family to please God and not man. They must be sure you are protecting and promoting God's interest and not yours or anyone else's.

A bigger picture of a purpose driven family were the Israelites. They were led by Saul. But when Saul failed and began to please men, God appointed David, a young man in his place. No wonder Job said wisdom is not in age or in gray hair. When a child has wisdom, the ability to know what to do and also do it well, he becomes the leader in God's purpose. Age is not relevant. A wise child can lead his family to God's purpose.

"Better is a poor and a wise child than an old and foolish king, who will no more be admonished." (Eccl. 4:13)

Gideon did exactly that, he destroyed the family idols and pioneered God's move. If you are a child reading this, the spirit of the Lord is coming on you to help you to destroy your family idols. It could be system and spirits that have intimidated your parents from God's purpose. You shall answer your parents' enemies at the gate. Get set, God is raising you to destroy your family idols.

No one is indispensable in God's program for a family. God can raise an effective leader to do His will, be careful so that no one takes your place. When a leader operates with wisdom from God, everyone complies willingly. When wisdom is not in place, the leader loses respect. In a home where mother or father is not leading in wisdom (word of God) they control by intimidation and manipulation even by cursing. If a mother or father or any leader is leading right, he needs not intimidate or manipulate. God's word (wisdom) compels a response from every member, just as the Israelites obeyed Joshua in all things.

"And they answered Joshua, saying, All that thou commandest us we will do, and whithersoever thou sendest us, we will go. According as we hearkened unto Moses in all things, so will

we hearken unto thee: only the Lord thy God be with thee, as he was with Moses. Whosoever he be that doth rebel against thy commandment, and will not hearken unto thy words in all that thou commandest him, he shall be put to death: only be strong and of a good courage."(Josh1:16-18)

Love is not optional when it comes to effective leadership. Love is God's wisdom to lead the entire family. You cannot love your wife and not the children or love the children and not love the wife also. You cannot lead outside the will of God and expects people to submit especially in this era of knowledge of the glorious gospel. I double check my leadership, when my children are unwilling to obey. You can only lead people but for so long outside the truth. Once the truth is discovered, you have lost leadership; they will stop obeying. As a follower, when it ceases to be as unto the Lord, check your allegiance. Do not let anyone lead you outside of God's purpose; taking advantage of you. Although the leader will give account and bear his punishment you are responsible to God for your life. Get mature by the word.

"And that from a child thou hast known the holy scriptures, which are able to make thee wise unto salvation through faith which is in Christ Jesus."(2 Tim. 3:15)

You are running a great risk if you have not discovered God's purpose, programs and plan for your life because you can be easily misled. Many destinies have been thwarted by the so-called "spiritual mother and "fathers'. If you read the accounts of the kings of Israel, some rose up against the ungodly influence of their ungodly mothers, and their thrones were established. Every throne is established in righteousness, even yours.

What am I saying? Examine every word under the crucible of God's word and purpose for your life. Let no one sow the seed of hatred in you because the seed will definitely grow and destroy you. Do not allow anyone sows tares (anything contrary to God's word in your heart). Only allow into your heart things that are in line with God's word. This is guarding your heart with all diligence.

> *"Keep thy heart with all diligence; for out of it are the issues of life" (Proverbs 4:23).*

But how can you do this if you do not know the word of God yourself? Do not just gulp everything you hear without examining it by the word. Because everything you hear has the potential to make or mar you.

Take heed to what you hear and how you hear. You can listen to everything but select the one you hear and let into your heart and spirit. No matter the source, check every teaching and make sure they line up with God's word. Like the Berean Christians, examine what you are taught with the word. Never compromise your faith and destiny.

> *"These were more noble than those in Thessalonica, in that they received the word with all readiness of mind, and searched the scriptures daily, whether those things were so" (Acts 17:11).*

Paul said in Galatians chapter 1 that, even I or an angel teaches something contrary to the knowledge you have received, do not be believe it. Refrain from teachings that will lead you astray no matter the source. Also, test the spirit and motive. If you keep you hearing garbage, you are not making progress in your walk with God. If you are not built, by the word you hear, you might have to leave the ministry.

A leader in the purpose driven family should understand that he represents God. Therefore let God's purpose and word rule through you. Do not embrace other purposes or it will steal, kill and destroy God's purpose for you. Do not expose your family to Satan's attack. Every purpose driven family leader should be subject to God's purpose and totally yield to His will.

Jesus is the effective head of God's family because he is always subject to the Father's will.

"Not my will but your will be done" (Luke 22:42).

Pride and ego should have no place in purpose driven family leadership. Be a God pleaser, not a man pleaser. A leader should be careful to lead correctly, or a stone be hung around his neck and drowned if any of these little ones go astray.

"But whoso shall offend one of these little ones which believe in me, it were better for him that a millstone were hanged about his neck, and that he were drowned in the depth of the sea" (Matthew 18:6).

"As smoldering flax he will not quench" (Isaiah 42:3).

Be careful not to quench potential or God's fire in the people you lead, but nurture them to greatness. Your word should be seasoned with salt (preservative) to minister grace to the hearers. You are in a position of influence, and a word spoken carelessly can crush a great dream or fire (zeal).

A purpose driven family leader should always say 'not my will, but God's will be done.' If it gives God praise and glory, I am all for it. Not my praise but God's praise. I have been crucified with Christ though I live not I, Christ lives in me.

> *"I am crucified with Christ: nevertheless I live; yet not I, but Christ liveth in me: and the life which I now live in the flesh I live by the faith of the Son of God, who loved me, and gave himself for me" (Galatians 2:20).*

All I am and have is to give him glory. When a leader has this attitude, he leads right and gets a good response of:

1.   Love

2.   Obedience

3.   Honour

4.   Prayer etc., from the people he leads.

CHAPTER 3

Communication In Purpose Driven Family

I n the previous chapter, we pointed out that the cardinal role of a leader in the purpose driven family is to get a word from the Lord and relay it to the people. In this chapter, I shall be elaborating on communicating the message to the people. When a leader gets a message and does not communicate it to the people, it is useless, because the message is meant for the people. Therefore, a leader must be skillful in the art of communication or his leadership will be compromised.

God holds a leader responsible for the message he does not relay to the people. As a leader, can God count on you to accurately relay His messages to the people or person it is meant for? I tell you, not every message of God is acceptable, but you must choose to relay it anyway. For the word of God is also for correction, warning, and instruction.

> *"All scripture is given by inspiration of God, and is profitable for doctrine, for reproof, for correction, for instruction in righteousness" (2 Timothy 3:16).*

When love is in your heart, you will find a way to communicate it well. Have love in your heart, and you will find the appropriate way to relay a message. A good leader must resolve to relay the message no matter what.

> *"And Samuel told him every whit, and hid nothing from him. And he said, It is the LORD: let him do what seemeth him good. And Samuel grew, and the LORD was with him and did let none of his words fall to the ground. And all Israel from Dan even to Beersheba knew that Samuel was established to be a prophet of the LORD" (1 Sam. 3:18-20).*

A leader's responsibility is that of a watchman that guards the city and blows the trumpet in case of danger.

> *"Again the word of the Lord came unto me, saying, Son of man, speak to the children of thy people, and say unto them, When I bring the sword upon a land, if the people of the land take a man of their coasts, and set him for their watchman: If when he seeth the sword come upon the land, he blow the trumpet, and warn the people; Then whosoever heareth the sound of the trumpet, and taketh not warning; if the sword come and take*

him away, his blood shall be upon his own head. He heard the sound of the trumpet, and took not warning; his blood shall be upon him. But he that taketh warning shall deliver his soul. But if the watchman see the sword come, and blow not the trumpet, and the people be not warned; if the sword come, and take any person from among them, he is taken away in his iniquity; but his blood will I require at the watchman's hand "(Ezek33:1-6).

A leader communicates God's word and purposes positively to avoid imminent danger and default to destiny. It is the leader's responsibility to say and yours to understand, accept and obey. A leader should pass the message in such a way to initiate the expected response from the hearers. Effective communication keeps every PDF member on the track and on the same page. It makes the task easy.

"And the whole earth was of one language, and of one speech. And it came to pass, as they journeyed from the east, that they found a plain in the land of Shinar; and they dwelt there. And they said one to another, Go to, let us make brick, and burn them thoroughly. And they had brick for stone, and slime had they for morter. And they said, Go to, let us build us a city and a tower, whose top may reach unto heaven; and let us make us a name, lest we be scattered abroad upon the face of the whole earth. And the Lord came down to see the city and the tower, which the children of men builded. And the Lord said, Behold, the people is one, and they have all one language; and this they begin to do: and now nothing will be restrained from them, which they have imagined to do" (Gen. 11:1-6).

Note: Communication is between God and the people, but He uses the leader as His mouthpiece

> *"But the Lord said unto me, Say not, I am a child: for thou shalt go to all that I shall send thee, and whatsoever I command thee thou shalt speak" (Jeremiah. 1:7).*

> *"But when Moses went in before the Lord to speak with him, he took the vail off, until he came out. And he came out, and spake unto the children of Israel that which he was commanded" (Ex. 34:34).*

Therefore, every purpose driven family member should see the leader as talking on God's behalf to enable obedience. See your leader as someone communicating the will and word of God; what God wants to be done per time. You may not always understand and agree, but that does not change God's expectation of your response to His word. When it is difficult to understand, still obey and ask God for wisdom rather than refute or argue.

> *"And they answered Joshua, saying, All that thou commandest us we will do, and whithersoever thou sendest us, we will go. According as we hearkened unto Moses in all things, so will we hearken unto thee: only the Lord thy God be with thee, as he was with Moses. Whosoever he be that doth rebel against thy commandment, and will not hearken unto thy words in all that thou commandest him, he shall be put to death: only be strong and of a good courage " (Josh. 1:16-18).*

Your leader, the watchman, maybe your mother, father, sister, brother, etc. Thereby refuse anything that will prevent you from seeing him as God's oracle and embrace the word he speaks. You may not agree with him on secular issues, but not on God's word or you will be shortchanging your destiny.

> *"Wherefore lay apart all filthiness and superfluity of naughtiness, and receive with meekness the engrafted word, which is able to save your souls" (James 1:21).*

Leaders are also teachers of the word. Sometimes they may not expressly speak the phrase *"Thus says the Lord"*, as in prophecy, but teach from the word which is God's mind for your preservation. Accept it as God's word to you.

God's servants are to teach, rightly dividing the word of truth. Teaching the right word as relating to specific issues and concerns. These teachings shine light along the path of purpose driven family and keep them from stumbling. It is the leader's responsibility to warn; teaching and admonishing from the word so that you may arrive at your destination.

> *"He chose David also his servant, and took him from the sheepfolds: From following the ewes great with young he brought him to feed Jacob his people, and Israel his inheritance. So he fed them according to the integrity of his heart; and guided them by the skilfulness of his hands" (Ps. 78:70-72).*

A leader is expected to lead from the integrity of his heart; saying all that God has commanded.

> *"And Samuel told him every whit, and hid nothing from him.*
> *And he said, It is the Lord: let him do what seemeth him good.*
> *And Samuel grew, and the Lord was with him, and did let*
> *none of his words fall to the ground. And all Israel from Dan*
> *even to Beersheba knew that Samuel was established to be a*
> *prophet of the Lord. And the Lord appeared again in Shiloh:*
> *for the Lord revealed himself to Samuel in Shiloh by the word*
> *of the Lord" (1 Sam. 3:18-21).*

Never be weary of the word, nor of the Lord's correction. Incline your ears continuously to the word. Bow your ears to the word. To bow your ears to the word means to respect and honour the word; accepting instructions and orders.

God's dealing with purpose driven family is cross-generational. Therefore you are expected to pass the word you are taught and your testimonies to your children.

> *"And the things that thou hast heard of me among many*
> *witnesses, the same commit thou to faithful men, who shall be*
> *able to teach others also" (2 Tim 2:2).*

> *"As for me, this is my covenant with them, saith the Lord; My*
> *spirit that is upon thee, and my words which I have put in thy*
> *mouth, shall not depart out of thy mouth, nor out of the mouth*
> *of thy seed, nor out of the mouth of thy seed's seed, saith the*
> *Lord, from henceforth and for ever" (Isaiah 59:21).*

There is a time to teach and a time to be taught. When it is your time to teach and lead, let the communication flow to the next generation. One person shall serve him, and it shall be counted as a generation. God has a generational plan for the purpose driven family that is why he is God of Abraham, Isaac, and Jacob. If Isaac did not pay attention to Abraham, his father, he would not have passed on the covenant terms accurately to Jacob, and God's purpose would have been jeopardized. I believe the reason there was purpose loss in Eli's family was poor communication.

I do not think Eli put enough emphasis on communicating the word. The mark of a good leader is effective communication that gets the attention of everyone on board so that Gods purpose will continue after him.

The Leader rules by the word. Do not neglect the sharing of the word in your home. It is the word that works on men and gets them to God's purpose. By strength shall no man shall prevail. It is my prayer that this work of God does not end with me. That my children will continue in their various future homes, even unto the fourth generation and more. So that God will establish his covenant with generations after me.

God's promises to you do not end with you. Teach your children His ways so He can fulfil the promises to them as well. This is the reason I teach my children the word daily; transferring God's spirit and word upon me to them for God's purpose.

"As for me, this is my covenant with them, saith the LORD; My spirit that is upon thee, and my words which I have put in thy mouth, shall not depart out of thy mouth, nor out of the mouth of thy seed, nor out of the mouth of thy seed's seed, saith the LORD, from henceforth and forever" (Is. 59:21).

Communication makes everyone's way level. Communicating God's word in the purpose driven family is like the light that directs and prevents people from stumbling. For he that walks in light has no occasion to stumble. *(1 John 2:10).* Stop the word; switch off the light, and people will stumble and falter. Communicate God's word to the people, and also communicate people's word to God. Obey your leader so that his communication to God on your behalf will be a thing of joy.

CHAPTER 4

WORSHIP:
Purpose Driven Family's
Power Against the Devil

"Therefore rejoice, ye heavens, and ye that dwell in them. Woe to the inhabiters of the earth and of the sea! For the devil is come down unto you, having great wrath, because he knoweth that he hath but a short time. And when the dragon saw that he was cast unto the earth, he persecuted the woman which brought forth the man child. And to the woman were given two wings of a great eagle, that she might fly into the wilderness, into her place, where she is nourished for a time, and times, and half a time, from the face of the serpent."And the serpent cast out of his mouth water as a flood after the woman, that he might cause her to be carried away of the

flood. And the earth helped the woman, and the earth opened her mouth and swallowed up the flood which the dragon cast out of his mouth. And the dragon was wroth with the woman, and went to make war with the remnant of her seed, which keeps the commandments of God, and have the testimony of Jesus Christ" (Rev.12:12-17).

PDF lives in the world where the enemy patrols and attacks. As soon as a family begins to serve God, she becomes apparent to the devil, and he begins to attack her to stop her from serving God's purpose. God has given PDP power to wage war against the devil and withstand him.

This power is worship. Family worship is God's strategy for PDF against the enemy. When PDF worship God together, they experience God, and His nature is impacted on each member. God's nature and power come on them which is a dynamic force to keep them advancing against the wiles and opposition of the enemy. Worship is more than mere singing songs; it is a life of total dedication and obedience to God.

"Sacrifice and offering thou didst not desire; mine ears hast thou opened: burnt offering and sin offering hast thou not required. Then said I, Lo, I come: in the volume of the book it is written of me, I delight to do thy will, O my God: yea, thy law is within my heart. I have preached righteousness in the great congregation: lo, I have not refrained my lips, O Lord, thou knowest. I have not hid thy righteousness within my heart; I have declared thy faithfulness and thy salvation: I have not

concealed thy lovingkindness and thy truth from the great congregation. Withhold not thou thy tender mercies from me, O Lord: let thy lovingkindness and thy truth continually preserve me" (Psalms 40:6-11).

This is a life that is sold out completely to God. When the entire family is sold out completely to God, keeping an unbroken relationship with God, obeying what He says, they move forward in God's purpose irrespective of what Satan is doing. Word zone is the only safe environment for PDF; which is the environment of worship. The devil fears when every member of the family is totally sold out to God in worship, because they will be united in mind and purpose, resisting him.

"Two are better than one; because they have a good reward for their labour. For if they fall, the one will lift up his fellow: but woe to him that is alone when he falleth; for he hath not another to help him up. Again, if two lie together, then they have heat: but how can one be warm alone? And if one prevail against him, two shall withstand him; and a threefold cord is not quickly broken" (Eccl 4:9-12).

The devil has no problem when any or some family members are left behind because as long as he got those ones, he can affect the rest.

You resemble who you worship, so when the entire family worships God, they resemble God, crushing the kingdom of darkness. Worship is very potent against the devil, and he will do everything to stop it. If he does that, family members will have different views on issues, not agreeing and as we all know, any house divided against itself cannot stand. The family in this state is already defeated before the battle.

In a situation where parents stay at home and children go to church or vice versa, the family is already defeated regarding God's purpose. The effect of worship is fully maximized when everyone is on board.

This is the reason Pharaoh was negotiating with Moses to allow the children to stay back. When family members have a different belief system, they are already defeated. This is why families are encouraged to attend the same church and be fed the same spiritual food; hearing the same word of God.

After you have magnificently experienced God in a worship service, and you return to the rest of the family, or to a spouse who was at home and did not share in the experience, you are drained and rendered ineffective, remaining at the same level and wasting the experience designed to move you forward. If you want to advance in the things of God, start believing God for the salvation of your entire family and corporate with Him.

"I and my household we will serve the Lord" (Joshua 24:15).

Before we consider the devil's strategies against family worship, let us look at ways to promote family worship; ways to provoke every member to be sold out to God.

Family Altar

- Set a convenient time of the day you can be in God's presence as a family singing, praying and sharing the word.

- Attend a full gospel living church

- Corporately seek God's will

- Serve God together

Let us examine the devil's strategies against family worship from Exodus *8:25-28, Exo.10:8-11, 24-26*.

These were Moses encounter with Pharaoh when God sent him to deliver the Israelites. We shall examine Pharaoh's various negotiations and relate it to family worship to stand against them.

Pharaoh Negotiated With Moses To:

- Worship God in his land of Egypt

The devil does not mind you having a relationship with God in his own land, on his own terms, where he rules. Because he is the ruler, he can dictate to you how to worship and what to worship with. In order words "worship God, but I shall tell you what to do."

His paramount goal is to dictate to you how to treat your family and spouse. Worshipping God but yet living according to the world standard. The devil is not threatened by such worshippers; he got them under his control. They profess to have a relationship with God but denying God's power. This is living under the law of sin which eventually leads to death. It is worshipping God with unregenerated mind.

When you worship in the land of Egypt, the devil has a major hold on your relationship with God. That's not worshiping, and it is unacceptable to God. You cannot claim to have a relationship with God and still live by the world's standard. Worshipping in the land of Egypt sounds like; 'it's okay to have sex outside marriage.' 'It's okay to cheat, everyone does it.' Worship at Satan's terms is being yoked with the devil who takes you nowhere. Do not bother worshiping God if you are unwilling to quit the devil's land.

A true worshipper living by the world standard is vulnerable to the attacks of the devil. This is the major reason there is no evidence of worship in most lives. Majority bear a Christian name, but their lifestyles are not different from the world.

Consequences Of Worshiping God In A Strange Land

- Your worship is detestable to the world

- You will be stoned by the people

When you profess to be a worshipper of God and people see no difference in your character, you become detestable to them.

They will mock you and ridicule God. Today many professed Christians have brought reproach to the name of God.

When you are detested you will be stoned, inflicted with trouble and pains. Persecution is associated with Christianity but be alert when it happens every time and from everyone. Joyce Meyer says check your obedience when you always have bad days. For your safety and honour, do not worship God in the land of Egypt (world system). God wants to take you to a land where He is the ruler and the Lord. That is why He says you should come out from amongst them.

> *"Be ye not unequally yoked together with unbelievers: for what fellowship hath righteousness with unrighteousness? and what communion hath light with darkness? And what concord hath Christ with Belial? or what part hath he that believeth with an infidel? And what agreement hath the temple of God with idols? for ye are the temple of the living God; as God hath said, I will dwell in them, and walk in them; and I will be their God, and they shall be my people. Wherefore come out from among them, and be ye separate, saith the Lord, and touch not the unclean thing; and I will receive you. And will be a Father unto you, and ye shall be my sons and daughters, saith the Lord Almighty" (2 Cor. 6:14-18).*

Leaving the land of Egypt is the first prerequisite for acceptable and effective worship. For the kingdom of God bears the seal, therefore, PDF must eschew all forms of evil and cleave to God's standards and righteousness.

> *"Let those that mention the name of the Lord depart from iniquity" (2 Tim. 2:19).*

God has a specific land he wants people to worship in. He has standard. He wants your worship to be a lifestyle than a myth.

> *"I beseech you therefore, brethren, by the mercies of God, that ye present your bodies a living sacrifice, holy, acceptable unto God, which is your reasonable service. And be not conformed to this world: but be ye transformed by the renewing of your mind, that ye may prove what is that good, and acceptable, and perfect, will of God" (Rom12:1-2).*

God wants our worship of Him to reflect in every area of our lives. Worshiping God without a lifestyle to suit is a waste of time and resources because it will command no power or blessing. Since God seeks relationship, He is holy and cannot tolerate sin. That is why the vessels that bear God must be clean. God's love for holiness is seen in the book of Leviticus, His orders for priests and the people of Israel. Moreover, His sacrifice of His only son to take away sin shows his hatred for sin and love for holiness.

Worshiping God without a lifestyle to match denies you the power thereof. It denies you God's power for blessing and promotion. Your worship is not true or acceptable to God if you still talk to your husband or wife anyhow, talk to your children anyhow or to your parents anyhow. Until your worship of God is brought to the home level, the devil will continually have a field day with your family.

As worshippers of God, He has expectations that govern your relationship with members of your family. In your home, do not adopt the ways of the world where children talk to parents anyhow. Let the love of God (worship of God) affect your attitude and behaviour. Let it be the determinant. Let the love of Christ compel you. I want to behave this way because of the love of Christ because I love and worship God. That is when your worship begins to account.

You cannot say you love God when you do not love your brothers you see every day.

> *"If a man say, I love God, and hateth his brother, he is a liar: for he that loveth not his brother whom he hath seen, how can he love God whom he hath not seen?" (1John 4:20).*

The home front is where the true test of worship begins because it is not a big deal putting up a farce in the church or outside. God expects you to be governed by his rules in relating to everyone, especially people in your household. If you are a true worshipper at home, I tell you, your worship is genuine and acceptable to God.

You must do all it takes to worship God in the land He desires. Families that worship in the land of Egypt are not free from sin and self. They are under the dictatorship of the devil; destroying and hurting one another, fighting themselves.

> *"For where envying and strife is, there is confusion and every evil work"(James 3:16).*

By themselves destroying themselves. Fighting themselves and far from withstanding the devil's schemes and wiles.

Every evil work thrives in such homes such as addiction, immorality, adultery, etc. If you are still observing the ways of the land in your family, the devil is negotiating your worship to have you as minced meat. Respond like Moses and say no to him, and take a three-day journey far from him.

A three-day journey may involve repentance and renewing your mind by the word, studying the word to know and act the way God expects, breaking company with some acquaintances for a drastic turnaround. Rather than sing the Lord's song in a strange land weep and mourn, be free. It may be painful taking a three-day journey but do it anyway.

> *"How shall we sing the Lord's song in a strange land?" (Palms 137:4).*

Abraham had to leave his country (Land) and everyone to the land God showed him for his worship to be acceptable. You must engage in spiritual combat against the devil to leave his land and worship God in His own land. The only time worshipping God will release the power of God on you as a family is when every member brings it down to a personal level, honouring God with a lifestyle that is pleasing Him at home. *(Read Ephesians 5:21-6:4; 1Peter. 3:1-17).*

Endeavour to line up your actions with the word especially at home. In your obedience do not compromise or retreat. This is the next strategy of the devil against your worship.

Compromise

If the enemy sees you refuse to worship in the land, he brings another negotiation. "You can go but do not go far." Do not go too far. In other words, you can obey God, but you can still reference the land of Egypt sometimes, especially at challenges. You can put your hand to the plough and still look back.

> *"And Jesus said unto him, No man, having put his hand to the plough, and looking back, is fit for the kingdom of God." (Luke 9:62)*

No, it does not work that way. When it comes to true worship, you cannot have two reference points and move far. You need your eye to be single so that your whole body will be full of light. You cannot have light some day and darkness sometimes depending on what you are referencing. Does that not sound familiar to many of us? We love to do God's will, but there are times or issues you deal with using your old ways.

I tell you if you do not go far, you will still return some day, and it will nullify your past worship. When you decide to live, true worship forgets totally the strange land of Egypt and what it offers.

I tell you as far as the east is from the west so is God's way far from the world way.

> *"As far as the east is from the west, so far hath he removed our transgressions from us" (Psalms 103:12).*

The two lands are in no way close, and there is no common ground. Therefore any compromise is actually outside the land of God – the ways of God. Present with the body, the Bible says is absent from God. He is either Lord of all or not at all.

When you are handling issues the way that is comfortable for you, it is an obvious sign you are missing out on God. Most times what God asks you to do is uncomfortable. Abraham, I tell you, went far away from his land. Had he not done that, he would have been tempted to return. I tell you, your land has such a strong pull. People tend to recline to the way that they feel more comfortable, feel they are in control and where they can predict the outcome. I tell you such ways could be manipulative and God detests that. God does not want us to manipulate one another but to allow His spirit access into our homes to influence every one unto His will.

When a wife or husband is displeased and resorts to denying each other conjugal rights to impose his or her will, this is manipulation. A child behaving in a certain way rather than God's word to compel mum or dad to respond is manipulation. Manipulation is a sign of witchcraft. Manipulation introduces the witchcraft spirit into the home. And tell me, how they can resist the devil? It is not your place to change anyone. It is the Spirit that changes people.

When someone does what displeases you, God's rule in true worship is to still love and pray for him or her. And God will move on your behalf to change that person. Love your enemies, do good to them that hate you. Do not repay evil for evil, give room for the vengeance and correction of God. *(Read Luke 6:27-36).*

When you go far from the land people will notice a clear difference in your behaviour. There will be no trace of your old ways. Never reference the land you left or what you used to be. God always has a word for where you are right now. Reference the word of God and move forward by the power of worship. I tell you, the devil will put many obstacles to make you reference the past so that you might return, but resist it. Forward ever, backward never.

Make a conscious decision to abide by the rules of the new country/land no matter what. When my family and I relocated to America from Nigeria, there were rules in America that were new and uncomfortable to me, especially the traffic rules. But for me to remain and thrive in America, my new country, I have to learn and adjust. This is how every true worshipper of God should adjust and fit into the new land, or he will deport himself to his old country, the way it used to be, reverting to the old habits.

To enjoy the amenities and blessings of the new land, you must adjust to the new rules. It is no different in worship. Relationship with God has lots of benefits but not without conditions; you cannot afford to live anyhow. Nothing dies in the land of worship; relationships thrive, joy and peace abound, provisions are available. The reason things are dying around you could be because of your lifestyle that drives away the presence and power of God.

If you negotiate your worship, things will begin to die around you, for example, your vision, dreams, strength, and health. God wants PDF to be totally consecrated to him, going so far not to hear the voice of the enemy or the people of the land even when they scream, nor be influenced by them. God wants you consecrated to him, having no other god but him, no other reference but him *(Exodus 20:3)*. Only then will you manifest his power for all to see.

I tell you when you introduce God's power into your home it can accomplish things beyond your imagination, beyond what you can do by your strength or manipulation. If Jesus refused to die He would not have seen God's marvellous power. Not my will but your will be done. Try and see it for yourself. When you begin to live by his word His power will be effective in your life.

> *"By pureness, by knowledge, by longsuffering, by kindness, by the Holy Ghost, by love unfeigned" (2 Cor. 10:6).*

Your relationship with the family members should be modelled and controlled by your relationship with God, or you could end up destroying each other. The land of worship is very important to God more than the worship. The land consecrates your worship and makes it acceptable to God. God is more interested in your relationship with your wife than the tithe you pay or your service. A teacher in my Bible school once told us how God reprimanded him for talking harshly to his wife asking him to apologize before dropping his tithe. God is concerned with the minutest detail. He showed the Israelites the particular place to worship and offer their sacrifice even in the Promised Land.

It is not just enough to leave the land of Egypt, to belong to God's kingdom, you must relate exactly as He commanded. Not just saying the good things, but saying the exact thing God commands. It is not just speaking the truth, but speaking it as commanded. Sometimes God may have you silent and not confront your spouse even though you know the truth. This is sacrificing in the particular spot in the land.

> *"If Balak would give me his house full of silver and gold, I cannot go beyond the commandment of the LORD, to do* **either** *good or bad of mine own mind;* **but** *what the LORD saith, that will I speak?" (Numbers 24:13)*

God is into details and wants us to mature in our worship, doing it precisely and exactly. Not just only separating the evil from bad but also separating the goodly from the godly. Something may be good, but God does not want you to be involved in it to advance you in your worship. Move away from the goodly distraction and be dedicated to him as a family. If you must grow in your relationship with God as a family choose the godly things from the goodly.

"All things are lawful unto me, but all things are not expedient: all things are lawful for me, but I will not be brought under the power of any" (1Cor6:12).

All things are lawful, but not all things are expedient. When you are not troubled by many things, you will be consecrated unto God, and your faith will grow to the extent that God will use you. The essence of worship is to be a blessing to others. When you get to the level of worshiping God for who He is and not what He does or will do, then God can use you. God wants to count on you not just to speak His word, but to speak the appropriate word on every occasion, situation and to every person.

Abihu and Nadab, Aaron's sons, offered unauthorized fire before the Lord and were consumed.

"Nadab and Abihu had died before the Lord when they offered profane fire before the Lord in the wilderness of Sinai" (Num. 3:4)

Profanity does not go with worship. Be careful, or you will be destroyed. Profanity means scornful of sacred things, rating God irreverently. Be careful for this is the house of God; you should know how to behave. Do not scorn sacred things. Your assignment from God is sacred, revere it.

God demands seriousness from us in handling kingdom matters. Everything in the house of God is sacred, and also everything we do in His name. Do not joke about it. Coming late to the house of God is profanity. Be eager to worship God, and you will receive all the benevolence of worship.

> *"And Moses made haste, and bowed his head toward the earth, and worshipped" (Exodus. 34:8).*

If you take your secular job seriously, you should take your relationship and commitment to God even more seriously for an utmost blessing.

You should not keep God waiting for you at the appointed time of worship. Those that seek me early shall find me.

> *"O God, thou art my God; early will I seek thee: my soul thirsteth for thee, my flesh longeth for thee in a dry and thirsty land, where no water is;" (Ps 63:1).*

You may miss God by not coming early to worship; missing a word relevant for your situation that was spoken before you came in. Cultivate the habit of coming early to meetings.

God is committed and serious, so should also be his worshippers. The shepherd and the sheep that arrived early are watered before the rest. I tell you, whenever it is worship time, angels are dispersed, handing out presents to the early comers.

Profanity is also treating the word with contempt; not been serious with the word nor staking your life on it. Believe the word and act as if your entire life depends on it, and surely it does because you live by every word that proceeds out of the mouth of God.

> *"But he answered and said, It is written, Man shall not live by bread alone, but by every word that proceedeth out of the mouth of God" (Matthew 4:4).*

God does not waste time with people that are not serious and committed. Worshipping in the land God choose is so important that God says if you have an offering leave it and go back and reconcile with your brother then come and offer it. God is more interested in your lifestyle than in your offering. Obedience is better than sacrifice. Obedience allows God's power to flow for your blessing.

> *"And Samuel said, Hath the LORD as great delight in burnt offerings and sacrifices, as in obeying the voice of the LORD? Behold, to obey is better than sacrifice, and to hearken than the fat of rams."(1 Samuel 15:22).*

Real worship is a lifestyle more than mere giving. God wants you to give your whole life to him. *"My son give me your heart." (Prov. 23:26).* God is tired of burnt offering and lip sacrifice that has no godly lifestyle. You cannot be in the land of Egypt and worship God acceptably. You cannot be your best in Egypt (world) and be your best in God. You cannot worship two masters.

You must deliberately put off the ways that do not conform to the land of worship. It is so important that the whole New Testament deals with how you ought to conduct yourselves.

A worshipper in Egypt is no threat to the devil, he is under his power. It is powerless worship.

> *"And declared to be the Son of God with power, according to the spirit of holiness, by the resurrection from the dead "(Rom. 1:4).*

Jesus paid the price of power through real worship with his life. Now that he has brought you into a union (relationship) with God, how much are you willing to pay to maintain that worship? God spared not his only begotten son, but gave him up for us.

> *"16 For God so loved the world, that he gave his only begotten Son, that whosoever believeth in him should not perish, but have everlasting life" (John 3:16).*

How much are you willing to give up to worship God in appreciation. When a family is dedicated to God, the enemy has no power or place in them.

Jesus said *"The prince of this world cometh and found nothing in me." (John 14:30).* When the devil negotiates your worship, let your response be an emphatic NO. Never entertain his negotiation, or else, you deny yourself power over him.

Exclusion

> *"And Moses and Aaron were brought again unto Pharaoh: and he said unto them, Go, serve the LORD your God: but who are they that shall go? And Moses said, We will go with our young and with our old, with our sons and with our daughters, with our flocks and with our herds will we go; for we must hold a feast unto the LORD. And he said unto them, Let the LORD be so with you, as I will let you go, and your little ones: look to it; for evil is before you. Not so: go now*

*ye that are **men, and serve the LORD; for that ye did desire.
And they were driven out from Pharaoh's presence." (Exodus
10:8-11)***

Satan negotiates that the old, young and wives should stay out of worship, but only the men should worship. We see that today in families, the children are not committed to the things of God, they are excused from it.

PDF worship is generational and should be passed unto the next generation. When the devil keeps the children and wives away, he stops the plan of God for the family. Eli suffered this. Everyone, both young and old should be involved in worshipping God, even in the family altar.

> *For I know him, that he will command his children and his household after him, and they shall keep the way of the LORD, to do justice and judgment; that the LORD may bring upon Abraham that which he hath spoken of him. (Gen. 18:19)*

> *"As for me, this **is my covenant with them, saith the LORD;
My spirit that is upon thee, and my words which I have put
in thy mouth, shall not depart out of thy mouth, nor out of the
mouth of thy seed, nor out of the mouth of thy seed's seed, saith
the LORD, from henceforth and forever." (Isaiah59:21)***

No one should be left out; your children are not too young to establish intimate relationships with God. Never excuse them to behave like their peers in the world. They are to be different in their lifestyle.

"Train up a child in the way he should go so when he grows up he will not depart from it" (Prov. 22:6).

If you do not involve them now, it will be too late for them to worship God later.

Children in PDF should not dress like their peers. Encourage good ethical code of worship. One time we went shopping for hair, my youngest daughter picked a weird colour; we stopped her and explained to her that she must be different so that her peers will have no problem seeing Jesus in her.

"Come out of them, be ye separate" (2 Cor. 6:17).

Dressing is good but should not mar the One we claim to worship. Our dressing should not detriment our worship.

There is dressing for the land of Egypt, even dressing of a prostitute, and dressing that befits worshippers, so choose wisely. Dressing should confer honour, dignity, and glory to you and not debase you. If your nakedness is shown, it is no longer glory and honour. Do not let trend debase you. You are not displaying for sale, but packaging yourself in a manner that brings honour to your Lord.

Doing all things as unto the lord. *(Col. 3:23)* You are redeemed as kings and priests to worship God. God gave instructions that the dressing of the Priests and Kings should be for glory and beauty. As a priest and worshipper, God is interested in what you wear. You have to please Him by what you wear. God wants your dressing to speak glory and beauty not seduction.

In as much as your dressing should not be seductive, it has to be beautiful. God is not pleased with old raggedy and worn out clothes and damaged shoes. You can come as you are but not remain the same.

Worship also affects the relationships we keep, the books we read, the movies we watch, and the businesses we do, etc. Children should not be left on their own while you go to worship. Take them to church. Let them experience the goodness of God. Train them in worship, reading the word, obeying the word and serving God. No child should be left out. If the devil gets any of your children, you will not go far, but return to Egypt.

> *"Let the children come to me for such is the kingdom of God"*
> *(Matthew 19:14).*

Resources

Not to worship God with your resources is the devil's final negotiation. *(Exo.10:24-28)*. This last time Pharaoh told Moses to go with the Israelites but to leave their herds, flock and cattle back in Egypt. Moses refused.

Worship is not complete and genuine without the willingness to surrender your substance. No true worship that will not cost you. If you do not worship God with your substance, surrendering all and be willing to do whatever He says with your money, your worship is not genuine.

Today some families have no problem worshipping God but have left their resources out. They worship God but are not committed to God and his kingdom financially. They do not obey God with their substance. As a result, they do not experience God's power in their finances. Until you give your resources in worship, the power of God cannot multiply it and increase your family financially.

The family that does not worship God with their resources will be under the attack of Satan. Their resources are still in Egypt, at the will of Satan. Until you are free in your finance, you are still bound to money answers all things. Anyone that has your money controls you; for where your treasure is there your heart is also.

"For God so loved the world, that he gave his only begotten Son, that whosoever believeth in him should not perish, but have everlasting life" (Matthew 6:21).

This is the situation of any family that does not obey God in their finances. They claim to worship God, but their heart is not with him. If you still struggle to give when the Holy Spirit nudges you, then you are not completely delivered. If you are worshipping with the whole of your resources, giving would be a delight. "We do not know the one our God will demand." The heart should be disposed to give whatever God demands.

A heart of worship considers nothing too big to sacrifice to God. He goes beyond paying tithe and offering. How many worshippers pay tithe even after a convicting bible teaching?

Until your finances are unreservedly involved, you are not truly liberated. You need to worship with your resources so that God's power will fall on it, multiply it and move you forward. Do not give people the opportunity to mock your worship for your poverty due to your reluctance to worship with your resources.

I break Pharaoh's grip over your resources. I blot out every reason and excuse the devil is using to stop you from giving offering and paying your tithe. These are his strategies to gain and exercise control over you. It is not your finances he is interested in but you. Because if he controls your finances, he controls your heart and you cannot go all the way as God intended for you.

This is the major reason Christians backslide; lack and poverty. The devil stops them from giving. As a result, they are not blessed, and in frustration, they turn away from God. Get your heart, soul, and body in true worship; learn to obey God in your finances. Can you obey when God nudges you to give more than your regular offering? Do not miss the opportunity for you to be blessed.

Give the Holy Spirit free control of your money. If He is not in control, then the devil is. And that, for him, is to steal, to kill and to destroy. When God is in control of your money as you obey him with your money, he multiplies it. Every command to give is an opportunity to be blessed beyond your imagination. Be in control of your money and deny your blessing. Let God control your finances.

Negotiation with your resources is the devil's final straw. Nothing opens a life to attack than financial lack. When you withstand it, you have escaped the devil's onslaught and territory. I will not give to my God that which cost me nothing. See what David said in 2 Samuel 24:24. A heart of worship does not only give when it is convenient, but it also gives at all times because he or she trusts God to send increase.

> *"And the king said unto Araunah, Nay; but I will surely buy it of thee at a price: neither will I offer burnt offerings unto the Lord my God of that which doth cost me nothing. So David bought the threshingfloor and the oxen for fifty shekels of silver" (2 Samuel 24:24).*

Your family cannot lack when you worship God with your money. Doing what He wants you to do with your resources. This also means prudent spending. If the devil is in control of your finance, he not only stops you from giving to God but makes you spend it on frivolous and worthless things, e.g. latest fashions and trends.

Though God wants you to look good, I do not think He will lead you to spend your money buying every fashion in vogue. God is prudent. He wants you properly fed but not wasteful. Do we not sometimes buy more than what we need as a family, food, clothes, etc.? God would have us save that money or invest it.

We should not be driven by our lust for the good things of this world, for everything in this world will pass away, and the money wasted. Be functional in your spending.

"Godliness with contentment is a great gain." (1 Tim. 6:6).

Do not be crazy about cars and buy every new model even when it is not necessary and financially wise. God is interested in your comfort but be moderate. The fact you can afford it does not mean you should have it or in the quantity you want.

God might have you buy two suits rather than five and channel the extra money to the kingdom or somewhere else that brings Him more glory. Worshipping God with your finance is realizing he is the owner of your money, not only your tithe and offering, and allowing him control over your spending.

Holy spirit how do you want me to spend this money? How many dresses should I buy? How much should I budget for this or that? I tell you, if you follow His budget even though it seems not enough, He will make it up for you.

The Holy Spirit had stopped me several times from buying things I needed and to put the money into the kingdom, and in such times, He raised people to buy those things that I needed. Worshipping God with your finances is to be sensitive to His voice on how to spend His money you are privileged to be the custodian.

"The silver is mine, and the gold is mine, saith the Lord of hosts"(Hag. 2:8).

Kingdom work has stagnated because the money that God released for it is tied in people's wardrobes and garages.

Many homes have also not advanced because of their mismanagement of the fund that God provided. Allowing God to be in control of your resources is not only for the kingdom benefit but for your welfare and that of your family. God is interested in your family advancement as well as the kingdom.

If God says do not buy a single cloth, shoe or bag for the rest of the year, will you trust him enough to provide or keep the ones you have from damages? You better be set because what He says could be as strict as that. Will you be willing to bless someone you do not know with money when He prompts?

My brother-in-law shared with me how a stranger approached him to pay his school fees, and that God not only asked him to do that but to also find out from the stranger if he has a friend that needed help with his school fees. It was not convenient for him like it is for everyone to part with money but he did. To the glory of God, both strangers have graduated and are professionals today.

He obeyed because of the realization that the money he has is not his but God's and God reserves the right to use it the way He wants. That is a heart of worship. If God wants you to cut down your tastes will you say yes? Like I said before, you cannot be the best in Egypt and be the best in the land of worship. Some things have to go. The major sacrifice you have to pay in worship is in the area of having the Lord control over your finances. Will you be willing to give up a family holiday for kingdom investment? These are practical examples of true worship.

But I tell you, when God is the Lord of your resources as PDF, He will never watch it go down. He will always multiply it unto abundance and makes all grace abound towards you. You might be thinking this is too hard to do, but if your heart is set on true worship, He will make grace available to you.

> *"And God is able to make all grace abound toward you; that ye, always having all sufficiency in all things, may abound to every good work" (2 Corinthians 9:8).*

You may be thinking, I do not have enough, I am not rich. That makes you a candidate of His blessing if you let Him be the Lord (owner) of your finances. When it is in your heart, it won't be long before you have abundance. In fact, He wants to be Lord now when you have little so that He can make it much.

True worship is a relationship with God through Christ so that you can share in His riches. When you obey, He empowers you to make wealth (increase). Everything thrives in the land of worship because of God's presence, even your resources as you offer them in worship. I tell you, when you give your resources over to the Lord, the devil will not have power over it. Anything that is still too difficult for you to let go when God demands it keeps your resources under the power of the enemy. In this end times, God is transferring the wealth of the Gentiles to PDF, but your heart must be trained and ready.

He wants to break every control of the devil over your resources, only agree with Him. God wants you to own things and not things to own you. In true worship He wants only Him to own you. And this is the ultimate of true worship; freedom from everything and total surrender to God.

Are you willing to let go of anything the Lord asks you? If yes, then he owns you. The disciples in Acts 2:45 sold and parted with their possessions as part of their worship to God.

> *"And sold their possessions and goods, and parted them to all* **men**, *as every man had need."*

They Left All To Follow Jesus

Anything you cannot leave when God asks you breaks your worship and hinders you from following God. Do not allow anything come between you and God.

When you refuse to negotiate your finances you take the spoils for the wealth of the unrighteous is laid for the righteous. *(Read Mark 10:17-31).* If money determines your mood and action then you are not a true worshipper yet. Your bank account should not determine your mood or dreams.

> *"For the just shall live by faith." (Hebrews 10:38).*

In God you live, move and have your being. Your relationship with God should be your determining factor. As a true worshipper, people should not detect when your bank account is red or buoyant through your action, mood or spoken word.

In the land of worship it is the Lord that supplies all your needs. Your faith should be towards God not towards your money. You cannot serve two masters, mammon and God. Choose one.

> *"No man can serve two masters: for either he will hate the one, and love the other; or else he will hold to the one, and despise the other. Ye cannot serve God and mammon" (Matthew 6:24).*

If you serve money live and work for money and you will be limited in life. If you serve God, live His purpose.

God wants to free you from the control of money. Money should not determine your attitude to people. Know no man by flesh. How does losing a thing affect you? What motivates you? Money or God? God wants to free you from every control to serve Him without fear all the days of your life. When you give up all you have in worship, God will be all for you.

> *"My brethren, have not the faith of our Lord Jesus Christ, the Lord of glory, with respect of persons. For if there come unto your assembly a man with a gold ring, in goodly apparel, and there come in also a poor man in vile raiment; And ye have respect to him that weareth the gay clothing, and say unto him, Sit thou here in a good place; and say to the poor, Stand thou there, or sit here under my footstool: Are ye not then partial in yourselves, and are become judges of evil thoughts? (James 2:1-4)*

CHAPTER 5

God's Wisdom For Purpose Driven Family

Ahouse is built by wisdom. If a family desires to manifest all of God's blessings, every member should be willing to operate God's wisdom; God's word.

Proverb 24:3-5, Proverbs 14:1

The reward of wisdom is overwhelming. God operates wisdom. He created the earth by wisdom *(Proverbs 3:19)* and upholds it by the same. God expects you and I to operate His wisdom *(Matt.7:24-27)*. Until you operate the wisdom of God, your house will not be established. The wisdom of God is available to you through Jesus, you can access it. Unto the righteous light appears in darkness. *(James.1:5)*. You cannot afford not to operate the wisdom of God. The cost is irreparable. God resists the proud. (***Prov. 3:35, Proverbs 1:25-33***)

A proud person is someone who is full of his ways and not willing to accept God's way. Humility is not what you wear or do not wear, nor how you speak. Humility is the heart that is willing to accept God's wisdom and will. These are the meek that will inherit the earth and all of God's good promises. God looks at the heart and sees who is humble, who is willing to accept His word and make the expected adjustments. Humility of heart is the first step towards operating God's wisdom.

Humility is not in looks but in the heart. Therefore, do not let any man deceive you nor judge you. God knows the humble heart; if He sees one, He will promote Him. When a family is unyielding to God's word, they will not move forward. You cannot be analyzing and resisting the word of God and think you are humble. I would rather resist men's word and appear proud than resist God's word. I choose to be humble towards God for my lifting, being God's pleaser than a men pleaser.

A family that will thrive in God's purpose should be God pleasers rather than men pleasers. This is because no man can do for your family what God can do for you and your family. And when you please God, He can move men on your behalf. Only God's wisdom will establish your home in God's purpose. You will experience all kinds of calamity when you are outside God's wisdom.

David operated God's word and chose his battles his battles wisely. Through wisdom, you can scale the enemy's wall. Do not by your foolishness enter every battle. When every member is humble; willing to say yes to God and seek his wisdom like precious gold, then they are set to build and grow. Everyone member of PDF should seek wisdom because everyone is a builder. There is a role given to everyone to play to prosper God's purpose, and this can only be through wisdom. If it is home, you are building then wisdom is expedient. Everyone needs to operate wisdom not to frustrate the work.

> *"From whom the whole body fitly joined together and compacted by that which every joint supplieth, according to the effectual working in the measure of every part, maketh increase of the body unto the edifying of itself in love." (Eph. 4:16)*

The wisdom of God makes everyone of the same minds, having the mind of Christ. When everyone applies the word, they are of the same mind.

> *"And the whole earth was of one language, and of one speech. And it came to pass, as they journeyed from the east, that they found a plain in the land of Shinar; and they dwelt there. And they said one to another, Go to, let us make brick, and burn them thoroughly. And they had brick for stone, and slime had they for morter. And they said, Go to, let us build us a city and a tower, whose top may reach unto heaven; and let us make us a name, lest we be scattered abroad upon the face of the whole earth. And the Lord came down to see the city and the tower,*

which the children of men builded. And the Lord said, Behold, the people is one, and they have all one language; and this they begin to do: and now nothing will be restrained from them, which they have imagined to do" (Gen11:1-6).

The only way PDF can be one in language and speech that makes them effective builders is by studying and applying the word individually and collectively. The only language and speech that builds are that of the word and God's wisdom. God's wisdom is not only for the mother or father but for all in the family. Even in marriage, couples should be humble enough to speak the same language of God's wisdom. Thinking and speaking only what the word permits.

If we all study the word, we will all have one mind (thoughts and will), and one language (faith) and nothing shall resist us. Personal and collective bible study time is not negotiable in PDF. So every member must be willing to cut down on movies, sleep, telephone, etc. And get wisdom from God's word which is like precious gold (money) that builds the physical house.

Just like in some families every member works, even the children, to finance the home in PDF, every member should labour to get precious gold to build the family in God's purpose. Wisdom is what each member is expected to supply and make the house grow. If you do not supply wisdom by your words and actions, you are wearying every other person.

"For the labour of a foolish man wearies every one of them"
(Ecclesiastes 10:15).

As a PDF member, be careful what you say and the way you act because others are affected, and much more, God's purpose is affected. Any action (labour) outside of God's word and will for your family is foolishness. Only God's wisdom from His word builds your home.

The wisdom of this world is foolishness unto God and cannot build nor sustain your home. Labouring outside God's word and will, with the mind of building your home is a mere waste of time and resources. God's wisdom might seem slow, but it is sure. God's wisdom and word are what you are given to build your home, not experience, common sense, logic, customs, tradition, etc., so use it no matter how it looks or how you feel. What are the characteristics of God's wisdom?

"Who is a wise man and endued with knowledge among you? Let him show out of a good conversation his works with meekness of wisdom. But if ye have bitter envying and strife in your hearts, glory not, and lie not against the truth. This wisdom descendeth not from above but is earthly, sensual, devilish. For where envying and strife is, there is confusion and every evil work.

But the wisdom that is from above is first pure, then peaceable, gentle, and easy to be intreated, full of mercy and good fruits, without partiality, and without hypocrisy. And the fruit

of righteousness is sown in peace of them that make peace"
(James 3:13-18).

In this passage, two kinds of wisdom are described. Anytime you operate outside God's wisdom; not having the characteristic of purity, peace, consideration, submission, mercy, sincerity, etc., God is resisting you, and as a result, the growth of the family is hindered. Ask yourself, by my actions, and words am I a promoter or destroyer of my home? If you always speak fear and doubt you are destroying your family and hindering God's purpose.

God's wisdom and His word guarantee success in every area of your life. If you want to succeed in your academics, finances, health, etc., lay hold on to it or you will be hindering yourself. You have been redeemed into the kingdom of light, and the devil is so far from you. The devil can only thrive to the extent you allow him by your disobedience to the word.

> *"Wherefore lay apart all filthiness and superfluity of naughtiness, and receive with meekness the engrafted word, which is able to save your souls" (James 1:22).*

There Is No Alternative To God's Wisdom

> *"Where shall we go you have the word of life" (John 6:68)*

> *"How shall we escape if we neglect such a great way of salvation." (Hebrews 2:3).*

It is not another marriage or home you need to fulfil God's purpose and be happy but His wisdom. If you cannot build your present marriage and home by God's wisdom, you will definitely fail elsewhere you go. Wisdom is the solution to build a sustainable home, not divorce.

General Wisdom For Homes

God has specific will and word for different families but has general wisdom for all families to live by. This is seen in *Eph. 5:20* and *6:18* respectively.

> *"Giving thanks always for all things unto God and the Father in the name of our Lord Jesus Christ."*

> *"Praying always with all prayer and supplication in the Spirit, and watching thereunto with all perseverance and supplication for all saints."*

The devil deceives through subtlety and over-familiarity to the word. Identify and avoid every devil's strategy and resist every of his manipulation. God has endowed your family with so much grace that when this wisdom is applied, you will triumph. I resist any devil that blinds you from the word. Wisdom is the ability to do God's word without question. God not only wants you as PDF to fulfil His purpose, But He also wants you to remain together and not disintegrate. Anything that affects you staying and remaining together as a family will adversely affect His purpose. Amongst many reasons, God hates divorce because of its effect on His purpose.

This is why God has given His wisdom as a stabilizing tool for the family against every challenge and pressure. Wisdom is God's word as revealed by the Holy Spirit. Therefore, when as a family you are faced with a challenge seek God's wisdom and never handle it in your own way. God's way is the only thing that guarantees your security during the storm. Your own wisdom might seem good and right but not strong enough to withstand the devil's attack.

Operating God's wisdom as PDF simply means finding His will in every situation and doing it, which in turn secures your family. If you must stand against every challenge of the enemy, then what you think and feel does not matter. If you are interested in the establishing of your home, keeping it from crashing and manifesting the fullness of God's blessing then, be willing and ready to accept the wisdom of God.

Through counsel, you choose your wars. Consult the word of God when there are conflicting opinions. As the husband and father do not insist on your way or right, consult God for His wisdom. I tell you, if yours is PDF there sure will be lots of challenges on every side, so you must be skillful in applying the word. Marriage is so important in PDF. It is the foundation and bedrock. So husband and wife must be willing to operate with God's wisdom.

As husband and wife; mother and father in PDF know that there is a greater purpose hanging over your union. You do not quit simply because you no longer feel like it. For purpose sake, God will give you the grace to endure.

God's wisdom should be sought at all times, every day, in every decision and occasion. One wrong choice could be detrimental and delay God's purpose for you and for your family.

CHAPTER 6

Finance In Purpose Driven Family

Finance is very vital in every family. It is a means through which needs are met and purpose realized, for money answers all things – *Eccl.10:19b.* This is why finance is so important. The Good news is that God has made adequate provision for that.

In this chapter, we shall be exploring how God provides finance for the family to accomplish His purpose and meet their needs.

> *"Hearken to me, ye that follow after righteousness, ye that seek the Lord: look unto the rock whence ye are hewn, and to the hole of the pit whence ye are digged. Look unto Abraham your*

father, and unto Sarah that bare you: for I called him alone, and blessed him, and increased him. For the Lord shall comfort Zion: he will comfort all her waste places; and he will make her wilderness like Eden, and her desert like the garden of the Lord; joy and gladness shall be found therein, thanksgiving, and the voice of melody." (Isaiah51:1-3)

Our Example Is Abraham

Abraham and his family set out to fulfil God's purpose and had enough to accomplish it and met all their needs. In the end, they were blessed in all things. Abraham was so blessed through all his generation.

> *"And Abraham was old, and well stricken in age: and the Lord had blessed Abraham in all things." (Gen.24:1)*

When God called Abraham, He called him alone. He left everything for the place God showed him (***Gen.12:1-6***). We can see that the only thing Abraham had was God's word, but in the end, he was blessed. God is not particular about what you have to leave to fulfil His purpose. He may have you leave everything because he is sure that his purpose will bring everything back to you even much more.

> *"Then Peter began to say unto him, Lo, we have left all, and have followed thee. And Jesus answered and said, Verily I say unto you, There is no man that hath left house, or brethren, or sisters, or father, or mother, or wife, or children, or lands, for my sake, and the gospels. But he shall receive an hundredfold*

now in this time, houses, and brethren, and sisters, and mothers, and children, and lands, with persecutions; and in the world to come eternal life." (Mark10:28-30)

Therefore consider everything as dung if you are called to his purpose. Abraham left all. It is obvious that the only thing they had was God's word; the assignment and purpose.

We were not told God gave them money, but in *Gen. 24:1*, we saw that they increased and were blessed in all things, even to the envy of kings. That means the only thing that brought this wealth was the word (purpose and assignment). It was his obedience to the word God spoke to him that blessed Abraham and made him abound in all things. This is faith.

That means Abraham got all by FAITH; he got all by simply obeying what God had told him. This is to say that in God's word there are provisions for all you might need as a purpose driven family. Your provision is not in a bank account somewhere or in that job, town, city or nation, but in what God tells you to do.

Faith: obeying God's word (assignment) is your means of livelihood. Even as it is written in Hebrews 10:38; *"The just shall live by faith.* As a purpose driven family, your concern should be doing God's assignment the way God says it and supply will manifest.

Until Abraham obeyed; there was no supply. How many times have you folded your hands waiting for provision before embarking on something God is leading you to do? It does not work that way in the kingdom. Provision and supply lie in your obeying. Until the word is obeyed, there is no provision.

Abraham set out to sacrifice Isaac (accomplishing God's word) before he saw the provision. Faith is the means of livelihood. Faithfully obeying what God asks you to do releases your hands to obtain the provisions He has made available for the work He assigned to you.

> *"For the vision is yet for an appointed time, but at the end it shall speak, and not lie: though it tarry, wait for it; because it will surely come, it will not tarry." (Hab. 2:4)*

> *Jesus says "my meat is to do the work of Him that sent me and finish it." (John 4:34).*

Meat is enclosed in the work. No work, no meat. This is why Jesus was not stranded. He went from city to city preaching the word, God provided for His work.

As a PDF anything that stops you from the assignment, no matter how logical, denies your provision. Let your hands continuously be on the plough for your fruitful harvest. Be careful to do all that is commanded for your provision.

Every instruction of God is a potential dollar, so write it down and cherish it as you would the dollar bills. Do all that is commanded and get all the provision you will need. God of the vision is God of the provision. If God gives a vision, assignment, He will no doubt give the provision, for no man goes to war at his own cost.

As a purpose driven family, it is foolishness to be concerned about the assignment and the required finances. No, be concerned about the assignment and God will be up to His responsibility of sending provision. You cannot do your part, and God's or you will wear yourself out. Many have been wearied out of their assignment because of the enormous burden of finance. If the assignment is from God, He will provide for it.

Therefore, make sure that what you do per time is from God or you will be providing for yourself. God does not waste resources on what he does not approve. Save yourself some anxieties, worries and high blood pressure by doing it as commanded. As a purpose driven family, faith is your currency of trade and transaction, so handle it prudently.

When you obey what He says, He will bless and meet your needs. When you pursue what God has called you to do, He blesses you (*Mark 6:24-34*). Direct all your energies at His purpose, and He will bless you. The Levites (Israelites' Priests) had no land, their portion was God. That means, just as their other brothers plough their lands with every diligence; they too should plough God's will and purpose to plant and harvest.

God's purpose cannot be done lackadaisically and expect to experience supply. If you do not work, do not expect to eat. There is no supply for a lazy purpose driven family. When you strategize and go about your purpose with all diligence, there is no way you are not going to be provided for.

See what God told Abraham in Genesis 15:1;

> *"After these things the word of the Lord came unto Abram in a vision, saying, Fear not, Abram: I am thy shield, and thy exceeding great reward."*

This is the same thing God is telling your purpose driven family. Do you need a reward (supply)? Then lay hold on me, I am for you. When you have me, you automatically have your supply. When you please me, you will have me, and I will supply all you need each time.

The question now is, "how do I lay hold on God, my reward?" (*See Isaiah 40:10* and *Isaiah 62:11*).

God stated categorically that His work is before Him and His reward is with Him. That means, before you go to God for the reward, you must do the work first. Undone work eternally constitutes an obstacle in your path for reward. Clear the obstacle by your diligent commitment to your assignment, and you will lay hold on God for your exceedingly great reward. When you are rewarded, I tell you nothing you could have ever had or left to do the work will compare to what you get.

The reward that comes to you is exceedingly great. No comparison. God's reward (supply) will blow your mind.

> *"He is able to do exceedingly above what you ask, think or imagine by the power that works in you." (Eph. 3:20).*

Until the power in you is put to work, there is no supply from the Lord. God does not support laziness.

> *"For every labour, there is profit, but the talk of lips tendeth only to penury." (Prov. 14:23).*

No wonder a wise man's heart is on his right, and the fool's on his left. That is, whatever a wise man conceives, he puts to work. The position of the heart makes one wise or foolish. Like the wise virgins, only wise purpose driven families enter the abundant life God that has planned.

This is God's way of provision. This is the way God rewards PDF with Himself. When you do the work and please Him, He is more than sufficient for your needs. You will have more than sufficient and in turn be a blessing to others. When Peter laid down the net as Jesus commanded, he caught so much fish and distributed to others.

As a purpose driven family, it may seem you are in lack, but I tell you; keep at the assignment and shortly those that mocked and scorned you will be borrowing from you.

Note:

Abraham's blessing was not immediate. It was not a flash show. The bible recorded him blessed in all things when he was old and stricken in age. But never was it recorded he lacked. What I am bringing out here? As a purpose driven family, you may not be so blessed at the beginning, but if you are patient and keep at your assignment, you will prosper and be so much blessed at the end. But one thing you can be sure is that God will never forsake you. He will always provide for you, only open your eyes like Hagar to see it.

You may start small; having left all to follow, but I tell you, your latter days shall greatly increase. As a purpose driven family, choose God and not money. Rather than to complain, focus on the purpose.

In Abraham's life, time and phase were everything. Every calling and purpose of God has the promise of great reward at the end. Therefore, do not despise your humble beginning.

> *"For who hath despised the day of small things? for they shall rejoice, and shall see the plummet in the hand of Zerubbabel with those seven; they are the eyes of the Lord, which run to and fro through the whole earth." (Zechariah 4:10)*

Do not be distracted nor give up. Resist every distraction due to your seemingly present lack. Be content and make the best of every provision. Make the best of the money He provided through comprehensive budgeting and management. Life is not in the abundance of riches but on the realization of God's divine purpose.

"And he said unto them, Take heed, and beware of covetousness: for a man's life consisteth not in the abundance of the things which he possesseth." (Luke 12:15)

Your life is much more than the food you eat, clothes you wear, the pleasure you get or any other thing this life affords. Your family is created for God's pleasure, and glory so, live purposefully. When you live purposefully and give God pleasure, you will find your pleasure. (*Job 36:11. Isaiah 27:2-3)*

Pursue God and not money or people. Embrace God your exceedingly great reward for all you need. God is worth more than you ever needed or desire.

Patience, contentment, faith, and commitment are the overcoming tools. They will keep you on track to obtain all that God has for you.

"Godliness with contentment is great gain." (I Tim. 6:6)

God had the promise of milk and honey for the Israelites, but at the beginning, He fed them with manna. In the wilderness on the route to the Promised Land, they only had their basic needs met. This did not invalidate the fact that there was abundance at the end. As a purpose driven family, there is usually a phase in which only your basic needs are met even at the minimum. Your provision is just functional basics. God supplies clothes just to cover you and nothing fanciful or expensive. This is definitely, not your best choice regarding style. When the Israelites were at this phase of life, the people that murmured at the provision died and could not get to the Promised Land. They exchanged their lives and glorious future for mere food. When you complain and despise any of God's provision, you are denied of the next and ultimately the abundant supply.

Man is not made for food, but food for man. The righteous man eats to live (eats for strength to do his work). While the wicked lives to eat; gluttony. It is important to realize that the purpose of life's is worth more than food.

Contentment gives you the right attitude to persevere until abundant rains of supply. As a purpose driven family, praise and appreciate God for every supply, and He will do even more. God does not abandon a purpose driven family, He always makes provision available. Only see and accept it.

Elijah was fed by a raven; he drank from a brook and kept alive by a widow and not some rich man. God is always faithful to provide; no matter the means, appreciate and accept it. Pride and greed, demanding more than is appointed at their current phase, has stopped some purpose driven families from accessing their provision.

The Israelites complained about manna, demanded quail, and God supplied but at the expense of their soul enrichment. They had quail in exchange for the prospering of their souls. They missed the process.

> *"And he gave them their request; but sent leanness into their soul." (Ps. 106:15).*

When I left my job for full-time ministry, my family and I accessed and appreciated each one of God's blessings. I taught my teenage girls to be grateful and appreciative of God's blessings and the means. Several times, we were blessed at our church's seasonal give away, by members of our ministry, friends, etc.

These provisions could either be brand new or used. Whichever and from whomever, we were grateful. This understanding made it easy working with every family member. We did not mind if we got a dress from a thrift store or a leading store. Like Paul would say in Acts 20:24; *"none of these moved me."* We have learned to abound and lack. What mattered to us is the assignment committed into our hands, not food nor clothes.

We consider the great work we are about and the work God is doing in us more valuable, and will not trade it for anything. God's purpose is our first consideration for every money that we received. It's now the custom to deny ourselves and invest into God's purpose. And each time, God provided for us exceedingly more than we could have afforded.

When you use all the money in your hands to eat your choice food or wear your choice dresses, you cut off your future supply. When you eat all your seed, there is no harvest for your tomorrow. What could have been a great future is buried in the bellies of people who ate the seed they could have sown.

As a purpose driven family, do not compare yourself with others nor be intimidated. Life is in phases as men are of different sizes. Do not compare your provision with another purpose driven family. Do not despise your day of small beginning or you will blow up your future. Accept and appreciate His provision for your family per time. Never trade your glorious future for mere provision.

Every of God's provision has seed to sow and bread to eat. Do not use the part you should invest as a seed into His purpose for food or you will be burying your future in your stomach. Wisdom is needed to efficiently manage provision to guarantee a continuous supply.

> *"Now he that ministereth seed to the sower both minister bread for your food, and multiply your seed sown, and increase the fruits of your righteousness." (2 Cor. 9:10)*

Organize and engage in programs that are within your means. Evangelism is evangelism, whether in your neighbourhood or outside your country. A purpose driven family chooses to sacrifice so that others might be rich. They deny themselves to invest in the gospel to make the benefactors rich. Understand it is your choice and be happy and bold about it.

CHAPTER 7

God's Reward System For Purpose Driven Family

For every labour there is profit. When a family labours in the purpose of God, there is a reward for them. Reward is God's idea for the purpose driven family. *"My reward is with me and my works before me,"* said the Lord of Host. *(Rev. 22:12).* When a family does the work (purpose) of God, they obtain the reward of God that is with Him. The reward of God is not without God. That means God rewards purpose driven family with Himself.

When you have God's presence in whatever you are doing, your reward is guaranteed, because the reward is with Him.

In other words, a purpose driven family should not seek the reward but God. When they find God, they have the reward. Do not bother about your reward if you have God's approval and grace in what you are doing. It is God's idea to reward purpose driven family.

He told Abraham, *"I am your exceeding great reward." (Gen. 15:1)*. The reward you will have for doing God's purpose is so much more; surpassing the reward you will get from doing any other thing. If you desire the best and most rewarding venture, then resign to God' purpose as a family. As a purpose driven family, you must understand God's reward system, how he rewards, or you will miss it altogether.

Ignorance is no excuse in the kingdom of God. How does God reward purpose driven family? Himself right? But how? Does He come in a form and dwell with you to reward your family? Now we shall see the means by which God rewards purpose driven family with Himself from the blessing Isaac blessed Jacob with. Isaac is in the lineage of Abraham's blessing.

Abraham's was a purpose driven family, and God blessed him. When he died, the blessing was transferred to Isaac. When Isaac was about to die, he transferred the blessing to Jacob. Let us see how he did it by exploring the content of the blessing.

In *Gen.27:27-29, 37-38*, Isaac blessed Jacob with the dew of heaven and fatness of the earth for plenty of corn and wine. Permit me to say that the summary (conclusion) of

Isaac's blessing on Jacob was corn and wine which is the only blessing he had otherwise he would have blessed Esau when he came. Corn and wine is God's rewards system for the purpose driven family. Since this is God's rewards system for the purpose driven family, you should understand what corn and wine mean.

Corn Signifies The Word Of God

> *"I am the living bread which came down from heaven: if any man eat of this bread, he shall live for ever: and the bread that I will give is my flesh, which I will give for the life of the world." (John. 6:51)*

"The sower soweth the word." (Mark 4:14)

Wine signifies the Holy Spirit.

> *"And be not drunk with wine, wherein is excess; but be filled with the Spirit." (Eph. 5:18)*

The Word And Spirit Are God

> *"In the beginning was the Word, and the Word was with God, and the Word was God." (John 1:1)*

Therefore God rewarding purpose driven family is with Himself; which is an exceedingly great reward, in other words, means God giving purpose driven family His Word and Spirit which does exceedingly abundantly above all they can imagine, ask or think. God rewards purpose driven family with a revelation from His word and pours His spirit to perform what the word says.

The word and spirit of God is the Anointing; the manifestation of God's presence. The word and spirit are all you need for any reward you need as a purpose driven family. It is not cars, houses, gold, silver, money, etc. you need; what you need as a reward of your service is His word and spirit, which in turn will provide beyond your needs. As a purpose driven family do not ignore the word of God nor neglect the Holy Spirit because that is the only means God rewards you. As God's servant seek His word.

> *"Therefore Eli said unto Samuel, Go, lie down: and it shall be, if he call thee, that thou shalt say, Speak, LORD; for thy servant heareth. So Samuel went and lay down in his place." (1 Sam. 3:9)*

> *"And now, brethren, I commend you to God, and to the word of his grace, which is able to build you up, and to give you an inheritance among all them which are sanctified." (Acts 20:32)*

In other words seek every blessing you desire in the word, find a word for it, and trust the Holy Spirit of God to bring it to pass.

"My mouth have spoken it, and my Spirit shall bring it to pass." (Isaiah 59:21). When God speaks a word concerning any blessing you might desire, His Spirit will bring it to pass. In

God's reward system, man is not the one that rewards you or brings to pass His promises for you. It is God. Do not cut ends to bring it to pass.

Every word (promise) that God spoke to the Israelites through Moses He brought it to pass by His Spirit. If you have found it in the word, rest assured that His hands will bring it to pass. Many purpose driven families have missed God's reward either by neglecting the word or not waiting on God to perform. If you do not study the word or wait on God to perform His word you miss the reward.

No man can do that which God has promised you in His word. You may be marginalized if you look unto man to do that which God has promised you. No man is qualified to reward purpose driven family, so do not make any man your idol.

> *"In the beginning God created the heaven and the earth. And the earth was without form, and void; and darkness was upon the face of the deep. And the Spirit of God moved upon the face of the waters. And God said, Let there be light: and there was light." (Gen. 1:1-3)*

The word and spirit came to play at creation to bring to pass God's desires. The spirit and the word work hand in hand. The word and spirit cannot work independently of one another in God's System. The word is worthless without the Spirit and vice versa. The Holy Spirit can only perform the will or word of God; if there is no word of God there is no performance. This is why many have died fasting and praying without the word.

The word does not perform itself. You may be a word bank, but without the Spirit, you will die without proof of the efficacy of the word. If you have God's word and spirit on a daily basis, you will have the blessing you desire every time. This is why it is important to have a study plan.

Rather than pursue blessing, go after the word and maintain fellowship with the Holy Spirit for performance. Through the word, you will discover what is yours, what is appointed for you and the Spirit performs it. This is the reward system. Doing God's purpose does not exempt you from seeking the word for your blessing, or you will be missing out on your blessing.

No wonder Samuel said, *"Speak Lord for your servant heareth." (1 Sam. 3:10)*. God's servants are entitled to God's word for reward. The word of God that tells you what to do is still the same that delivers your reward. As a servant of God, go for a double portion of the word for your assignment and reward. Do not only get instructions on what to do or what to preach but also get for your personal reward.

As you are doing the work, go to the word for your reward. Your word time as a purpose driven family should go above the ordinary level, or you labour in vain. If the Holy Spirit is this important for your reward, then reverence Him even at home. Do not grieve or quench the Holy Spirit or you will miss your reward.

> *"Neither say they in their heart, Let us now fear the LORD*
> *our God, that giveth rain, both the former and the latter, in*
> *his season: he reserveth unto us the appointed weeks of the*
> *harvest." (Jer. 5:24)*

As a purpose driven family, you cannot afford these; fights, lies, bitterness, malice, fornication, adultery, etc., or your labour will be futile. This is one of the reasons God's blessings are not seen in some homes. Adultery eats up blessings like fire. Avoid it. If you want your service to count, then practice His presence at home.

The blessing of Corn and wine was the blessing Samuel proclaimed on Saul after he was made King.

> *"Then shalt thou go on forward from thence, and thou shalt*
> *come to the plain of Tabor, and there shall meet thee three*
> *men going up to God to Bethel, one carrying three kids, and*
> *another carrying three loaves of bread, and another carrying*
> *a bottle of wine." (1 Sam. 10:3)*

May God bring into your life people that will give you bread and wine. Ministers equipped with the spirit and word for your reward. When you are blessed with corn and wine you are set to go anywhere, God might send you. The disciples were sent with nothing; no purse nor bag, but they did not lack. With corn (word) and wine (spirit), you are blessed anywhere you go.

What a portable blessing. It is easier carrying the word and spirit than land, houses, cars, etc. Therefore do not bother what you may have to give up doing God's purpose because the corn and wine will always produce on your arrival. You may not look it now, but I tell you if you have the word and the Spirit of God, you are loaded with blessing. Only allow time, and they will manifest. You are a bomb of blessing about to explode. Do not let anyone look down on you nor look down on yourself. Though your beginning may be small, your end shall greatly increase. You are too loaded, and very soon you shall appear in style.

> *"Let no man despise thy youth; but be thou an example of the believers, in word, in conversation, in charity, in spirit, in faith, in purity." (1 Tim. 4:12)*

There is no ceiling to your blessing because there is no limit to what the Spirit and the word can do. Never let your eyes and ears limit you for no eyes have seen nor ears heard what the spirit is up to for those who love Him. Your wonders are about to explode in Jesus mighty name. The things you see are made from things you do not see; the word and Spirit. You may not see it, but it is real and sure. If the beautiful worlds and all in them were formed by the word how much so less will the same word create your world with all you desire? All you desire for reward is already available via the word. You can call them forth by His Spirit. *(1 Cor. 2:9-16)*

May God send you ministers with His word and Spirit to multiply and preserve your blessing; destiny helpers. As purpose driven family select who you allow into your life. They should benefit you with the word. Keep the right associations. Your close associates should have and revere the word and Spirit of God to add to you. People you hang out with affects your blessing. If you hang out with people that distract you from the word, they will prevent your blessing. Avoid them and crave for the word.

When you labour to get the word and spirit, you will not labour for the things people seek after. Buy the truth (word), and you will not spend your time and money on things that perish with use. The price you pay for the word is the price you pay for your blessing. When you buy oil and anoint your eyes, you will see the blessing in the word. The oil that opens your eyes is the Holy Spirit.

> *"Open thou mine eyes, that I may behold wondrous things out of thy law." (Ps. 119:18)*

The book of Proverbs talks about the magnificent and enormous blessings in the word.

> *"All you desire cannot be compared to it." (Prov. 8:11).*

In other words, the word is exceedingly above your desires. You can outlive every famine and scarcity by corn and wine.

> *"And let them gather all the food of those good years that come, and lay up corn under the hand of Pharaoh, and let them keep food in the cities. And the seven years of dearth began to come, according as Joseph had said: and the dearth was in all lands; but in all the land of Egypt there was bread." (Gen. 41:35, 54)*

That means God's reward is not dependent on the prevailing economy. This is the only reward system that is sure. When you miss it, you struggle. After Esau missed it, he regretted.

> *"And Esau said unto his father, Hast thou but one blessing, my father? bless me, even me also, O my father. And Esau lifted up his voice, and wept. And Isaac his father answered and said unto him, Behold, thy dwelling shall be the fatness of the earth, and of the dew of heaven from above; And by thy sword shalt thou live, and shalt serve thy brother; and it shall come to pass when thou shalt have the dominion, that thou shalt break his yoke from off thy neck." (Gen. 27:38–40)*

Adam lost it and struggled, he was sent out of Garden of Eden, the word place. Choose one, do you want to be blessed by God via His anointing or do you want to get it yourself, by your strength. Then choose the price to pay. Labour in the word and Spirit or chase after "these things." I tell you no man that chases after wealth catches it, for riches develop wings and fly. By strength shall no man prevail, but if you pursue God and please Him, He catches the riches and brings them to your doorstep like manna.

Jesus the living word is our manna from heaven. He is our blessing and what we should seek. When you do, He will lead you out to pasture and make you lie down by the still waters. When the Lord is your shepherd, listening to His voice (word), goodness and mercies shall follow you all the days of your life. You can be blessed every day if you wait on the word daily. *(Psalms 23)*

This is God's reward system for tithers. When as a purpose driven family you pay your tithe, God opens the window of heaven and pours such a blessing for you. The blessing of Corn and Wine. That is to say, when you pay your tithe, God grants you inspiration in His word and pours out his Spirit to perform until there is not enough room to receive it. This is the reward system God has put in place.

> *"And now, brethren, I commend you to God, and to the word of his grace, which is able to build you up, and to give you an inheritance among all them which are sanctified." (Acts 20:32)*

Every reward is conveyed by the word. When you serve God, He blesses your provision, takes sickness away from you, fulfils the number of your days, destroys your enemies, etc. All these are conveyed by the word. As a servant of God, you should be wise to listen to the word for all your needs.

> *"How shall we escape, if we neglect so great salvation; which at the first began to be spoken by the Lord, and was confirmed unto us by them that heard* **him.** *" (Heb. 2:3)*

There is no other way to reward but the word. The majority are denied of blessing because they find no time for the word. If you praise, worship and pray, find time to get the word for the spirit to perform. Do not waste the spirit of God you carry, activate the spirit by having the word in your mouth and heart. You are born again by the incorruptible word of God; every blessing of your redemption is conveyed by the word. The word of God is like the brick the Holy Spirit uses to build your new life of abundance. The Holy Spirit manifests the word you discover the reason for building your new life; recreation.

No purpose driven family or church grows beyond the word and the Spirit, there is no blessing that can amount to it. Your strength may get you a house but not a home or protection. Your strength may get you food but not appetite. I tell you, the blessings of God make riches and add no sorrow *(Prov. 10:22)*. He increases and comforts you on every side. His blessings are good and perfect. Go for the word. God cannot do beyond His word in your life; as far as you can see the gives to you.

> *"If you abide in me and my word abide in you ask anything and it shall be done unto you." (John 15:7)*

This is the secret behind every purpose driven family that have been thriving in God's purpose. Do not envy them. You too can have what they have, only go for the word. The anointing is available to all only be willing to pay the price. People that choose not to pay the price envy people that have what they desire. They oppose and speak against the word because knowledge is too far from them.

Esau was angry with Jacob. *(Gen. 27:41)*. If you have the anointing, be careful of envy by people around you that do not have it. When as PDF you begin to excel in God's blessing because of the anointing, people will begin to envy you. To them, you easily have the things they are toiling far. Esau was angry with Jacob, and he planned to kill Him.

People that envy you will seek to kill you, targeting the anointing. They antagonize every word you preach to dissuade you from the word. Be careful of the Esaus in your life. They could be close to you as a brother, sister, and friend. You could be sleeping on the same bed with Delilah, or go to the same church with her. Identify the Esau and Delilah and keep off. Esau's are people in your life that do not care about their birthright (redemptive benefits). They do not explore their privileges in the word.

Esaus pay no attention to the word. They take the kingdom business lightly and oppose sound teaching. Esau's are worldly, concerned about themselves, their belly and red porridges (lust of the eye and world). For your interest when you identify any Esau, keep off no matter who he is. When Esau strives with you, do not quarrel with him. Keep a safe distance. Do not graze together. Abraham gave up his right and refused to quarrel with Lot. If you quarrel with Esau, you quench the anointing in your life. Never forget that Esau's target is the anointing, so guard it at any price. Do not let their attitude to the word affect you. Anyone that makes a mockery of God's anointing (word and Spirit) in your life hates you; you are better far from him. He is only seeking the opportunity to harm you when your anointing is low.

Esau could not kill Jacob as long as Jacob their father was alive. This is how the devil is helpless with the anointing; the presence of God your father in your life. The devil or his agents cannot do you any harm until God's word and Spirit in you is low. So do not attend to any Esau at the expense of God's word and Spirit. Do not be Martha who is troubled by so many things.

> *"And Jesus answered and said unto her, Martha, Martha, thou art careful and troubled about many things: But one thing is needful: and Mary hath chosen that good part, which shall not be taken away from her." (Luke 10:41-42)*

The word is all you need to quell every challenge and trouble. As a purpose driven family, maintain the right priority on the word and prayer or Satan will toy with you. Make the word and prayer your priority. The word and spirit is your safe environment. In the word environment, you are too protected to be molested.

Jesus said, *"The god of this world comes and finds nothing in me." (John 14:30).* Do not keep Esau close or they will lead you to sin like Delilah. Go as far as you can. The Holy Spirit will teach you how to be safe from Esau's by expounding the advice of Rebecca to Jacob. *(Gen. 27:41-45)*

1.   Keep off for a few days

2.   Go to Laban and tarry there.

Jesus told the disciples to tarry in Jerusalem until they are endued with power. Envy is a force, and you need the power to withstand it. When Esau arises, keep off, tarry in the word and His presence to be empowered to resist their vices. Joseph played into the hands of his envious brothers *(Genesis 37)*. Jesus knew what was in man and did not commit Himself to any man.

> *"But Jesus did not commit himself unto them, because he knew all* men, *And needed not that any should testify of man: for he knew what was in man." (John 2:24-25)*

Do not commit yourself to anyone. Love enough to be free. When you love to the point of enslaving yourself, you are endangering your life because when the anointing is destroyed, you will be destroyed. Love and yet be free to do the purpose of God. Love people but seek the word and the Spirit for yourself. Be committed to people and yet still find time for the word and prayer. The bible teaches there is time to hug and time to refrain from hugging. *(Eccl 3:8).* So not go too far from the word to please people, or you will die. Do the things only the word and Spirit moves you to do. There should be wisdom dealing with Esau *(Gen. 33:4, 12-16)*.

Respect Esau but be far enough to be safe. Respect them but guard your tender vision, dreams, and aspirations from them or they will destroy them. Guard your heart; be in control of your decisions by the word when dealing with Esaus in your life.

After the dust was settled, Jacob was wise when relating to Esau. Be led by the word and spirit as you relate to people that are envious of you. Keep the anointing steadily on for life, and you shall abound in God's blessing no matter who likes it or not. If nothing or no one stops you from pursuing purpose, then nothing is strong enough to keep you from the blessing, only BE WISE.

CHAPTER 8

Unity, A Stabilizing Force For Purpose Driven Family

Although Purpose Driven Family (PDF) is pursuing one purpose, they are not one individual. In other words, it's not about uniformity. PDF are related individuals coming together to accomplish God's purpose. The individuals have different gifts, calling, grace and personalities but pursuing the same purpose, contributing in different ways and at different points. Their differences are mostly due to the working of the Holy Spirit in them.

> *"But all these worketh that one and the selfsame Spirit, dividing to every man severally as he will." (1Cor.12:11)*

The Holy Spirit works in and through the individual members to produce individuals suitable for God's purpose as He pleases. Therefore it is absolutely not possible for all of them to work and behave alike. For if the whole body were the eye where will the hearing be?

> *"If the whole body were an eye, where were the hearing? If the whole were hearing, where were the smelling? But now hath God set the members every one of them in the body, as it hath pleased him. And if they were all one member, where were the body? But now are they many members, yet but one body." (1 Cor. 12:17-20)*

Uniformity makes every member to be an eye, which does not fulfil God's purpose. For the family to remain as a functional unit, there must be a proper understanding of these differences of personalities and gifting. Where more than one person is working to accomplish a purpose, unity is the name of the game and not uniformity. They are united in purpose but different in approach. They may appear different by their tasks and personalities but still accomplishing the same purpose.

Uniformity is acting as one person, having the same view, approach, ideas and operating similarly and doing the same thing. This is not God. Uniformity is not God's way of accomplishing His purpose, He is God of variety. God is the God of unity, not uniformity. God is three in one, having different functions.

Purpose Driven Families should understand this to accept and tolerate each other. Understand that your family is made for the same purpose but not the same person. The mother is not like father and children are not like their parents. And children are not all alike. Do not expect the other to respond and have the same view as you. Some are introvert, others extrovert. The good news is that when you yield to the Holy Spirit, He can work through everyone to accomplish His purpose as He wills.

When members of PDF appreciate their differences, love and tolerate one another, they remain together in purpose. The understanding of this is the stabilizing factor in accomplishing God's purpose. Unity gives the Holy Spirit full manifestation and expression resulting in blessing and advancement of the assignment committed to the family.

Unity enables you to draw strength from each other for success and compensates for any weakness.

> *"But the manifestation of the Spirit is given to every man to profit withal."* (1 Cor. 12:7).

When one falls, the other will help him up. The advantages of teamwork stem from unity. *(Ps.133:1-3)*

What is unity? Unity simply states, though we are different we still love enough to be together accomplishing the same purpose; marrying our gifts, talents, and personalities to accomplish

God's purpose. The family that must stay happily together should understand this principle. As you live and work together, you should respect and honour each other in love. Listen to and respect ideas and opinions even when they do not make much sense or differ from yours. Love, when demonstrated this way, draws God's presence to bless you and your work; commanding His blessing and life evermore on your family.

That seemingly unintelligent idea may be what you need to get the job done. If Naaman did not value his servant's idea, he would have remained leprous for life. *(2 Kings 5).* You may not like the idea but accept it anyway for the good of all. Allow the Holy Spirit free access regardless of your feelings.

PDF structure should be such that everyone is free to express what God is doing in them. No one should be hindered. There is one Lord, and that is Jesus Christ, who only should be feared. God expects you to love, honour and respect your parents but not fear them. Do not let fear stop you from doing what God says.

Uniformity is man-made in a bid to control, intimidate and control others. You are to dominate and subdue the earth not dominate fellow men. God does not want people to control people but His Spirit to lead them. Rather than try to control your children to teach them God's word, pray for them and trust God by His Spirit to lead them to the right choices.

"Train up a child in the way he should go, and when he grows up, he will not depart from it." (Prov. 22:6)

The problem is this, if you miss the required training, you will resort to control measures and intimidation.

Uniformity kills conscience and shipwrecks faith. God has a destiny for everyone; let Him lead them to fulfil it. When someone is compelled to work against his conscience, his faith is shipwrecked. Faith is everything to a believer; by it, he or she pleases God and obtains every blessing. What your conscience may allow you to do may not be comfortable to the other person, so do not impose or you destroy his or her faith. Let everyman see to what he allows. My viewpoints should not make you ignore your conscience or change yours unless the Holy Spirit convinces you otherwise. And while I wait for that, I should still love you and treat you respectfully.

Uniformity prevents you from fulfilling God's purpose and denies your full reward in Christ. I have seen families where everyone is forced to behave and respond to issues in the same way. Do not be partaker of another man's sin. Though you are united in purpose, everyone will give an account of himself to God. This end time is not for uniformity, but unity or you might miss God's plan, program, and heaven. Be God-willed, or you will be blown away by the wind. *(Luke 12:49-53, Luke 9:63)*

Any member that catches the fire of God should run with it regardless of who is coming or not. Obedience to what God is asking you to do is personal and not a collective venture. Though you are a member of your family, be personal enough to relate to God and obey Him.

"Just as you have received Him as your Lord and Saviour walk in Him." (Colossians 2:6).

Be strong willed to do whatever your Lord and Saviour convinces you to do. Everyone will bear his own cross and reap his own reward.

Sometimes there might be clashes of interest, wishes, and plans but look beyond those. The things that bind you are more than the things that divide you. How do you think Joseph and Mary reacted when they finally saw Jesus after looking for him for three days? It is an easier read than imagined!

PDF will be ineffective if members do not imbibe unity because all things are made for His purpose. This is a major reason divorce is on the increase. The family that will survive this end times onslaught is one whose members choose to honour Jesus as Lord by doing the will of God. The power of His will keep them together. Although as a family you are expected to fulfil a purpose as one PDF family, but in heaven you are crowned and rewarded individually. It is everyone to this own reward.

Everyone is expected to bear his own burden doing the will of God. This is to say that there might be clashes of tasks, wishes or plans in PDF but look beyond that to the bond of unity. How do you think Joseph and Mary reacted when they saw Jesus in the temple after looking for him for three days? When we read such thing it sounds light but off course it was painful.

What do you think was the reaction of Gideon's parents when one morning they woke and Gideon has destroyed the family idol? (Judges 6). What about Samson's parents and his choice to marry a Midianite woman, Delilah? (Judges 16). Can you have these varied opinions and circumstances in your family and still love enough to stay together and continue to pursue purpose; that's unity. Parents in PDF should understand they are mere custodians of children not owners. Our actions should be in check least we fight God and kick against the prick.

What happens when PDF is united? Jesus and the Father will come and make their home with them. *(John 14:23)*. No matter how humble your home might seem, their presence will make it beautiful and glorious and will attract people for you to bless, and they in turn will bless you. The presence of God will make it safe for children to live and thrive. There will be no quarrels, arguments and confusion. Divorce can never be mentioned in a home where Jesus lives.

His love becomes your life; a life of love, health, wealth and strength. His ability becomes yours and nothing can stop your home. You are united to prevail over every strategy of Satan the devil. As a member of PDF be secure in your very own assignment and never think you are inferior.

BLURB FOR BACK COVER

God's purpose for you is generational, involving every member of your family. Learn from this easy to read book how you can make it happen; getting everyone on board for their full reward. Psalm 22:30 paraphrased, one person shall serve Him and it shall be counted for him as generation. Get the key to generational service and blessing.

CHAPTER 9

Destiny Marriage: Purpose Driven Family Legacy To The Next Generation

Who you marry as a member of a purpose driven family (PDF) is very important if you must continue with the family legacy. As I said earlier, God's plan transcends generations. God's design is that one generation serves Him to the next. That is why the Levite's where instructed to marry from their tribes.

As a parent in PDF, who your children marry should be of utmost importance to you. Who you let into the ship of your family would, in turn, affect God's purpose for your family either positively or negatively.

Though you may not decide who they marry, you can influence their choice on your knees. Be spiritually alert and discerning to pick a signal from God concerning the choices they make. Nothing wrecks destiny than the wrong choice in marriage.

My desire is that after reading this chapter, you will be armed to choose right.

Definition of Destiny Marriage

Destiny marriage is God's ordained marriage between a man and woman that suits and fulfils God's divine destiny for your life (purpose and plan). It is the marriage that helps you fulfil God's vision for your life.

Not only are you a member of PDF you are God's creation for His purpose, like Jeremiah (Jeremiah 1:5). And if you are to fulfil His purpose and in turn carry your family legacy to the next generation, this topic is to be of utmost importance to you just like it is in the heart of God. God is seeking godly seeds.

> *"God wants husbands and wives to become one body and one spirit. Why? So that they would have holy children and protect that spiritual unity. Don't cheat on your wife. She has been your wife from the time you were young" Malachi 2:15 Easy-to-Read Version (ERV).*

I have preached at numerous marriage conferences, seminars and youth gatherings but have never gotten this revelation I am about to share. This is why I strongly believe that this message is designed by God to avoid an imminent catastrophe in someone's life.

If you are a man or woman of destiny with God's purpose in your life, then destiny marriage is for you if you are to fulfil that divine purpose. Destiny marriage is something you have to do consciously because it either makes or breaks you. You may be fulfilled and celebrated in every other area – career, profession etcetera but if you do not make the right choice of marriage – who you marry, you are ruined for life.

If the devil doesn't get you to make the wrong choice in marriage, you have escaped him eternally. But if he does, he has ruined you for life. So marriage decision is a decision you make consciously, informatively and with the help of many godly mentors and counsellors you have proved their counsel and ability to hear God in the past.

Essence Of Marriage

God's intended marriage to help a man fulfil his destiny.

Genesis 2: 8-25

"And the LORD God planted a garden in Eden, in the east, and there he put the man whom he had formed. And out of the ground the LORD God made to spring up every tree that is pleasant to the sight and good for food. The tree of life was in the midst of the garden, and the tree of the knowledge of good and evil.

A river flowed out of Eden to water the garden, and there it divided and became four rivers. The name of the first is Pishon. It is the one that flowed around the whole land of Havilah, where there is gold. And the gold of that land is good; bdellium and onyx stone are there. The name of the second river is the Gihon. It is the one that flowed around the whole land of Cush. And the name of the third river is the Tigris, which flows east of Assyria. And the fourth river is the Euphrates.

The LORD God took the man and put him in the garden of Eden to work it and keep it. And the LORD God commanded the man, saying, "You may surely eat of every tree of the garden, but of the tree of the knowledge of good and evil you shall not eat, for in the day that you eat of it you shall surely die."

Then the LORD God said, "It is not good that the man should be alone; I will make him a helper fit for him." Now out of the ground the LORD God had formed every beast of the field and every bird of the heavens and brought them to the man to see what he would call them. And whatever the man called every living creature, that was its name. The man gave names to all livestock and to the birds of the heavens and to every beast of the field. But for Adam, there was not found a helper fit for him. So the LORD God caused a deep sleep to fall upon the man, and while he slept took one of his ribs and closed up its place with flesh. And the rib that the LORD God had taken from the man he made into a woman and brought her to the man. Then the man said, "This, at last, is bone of my bones and flesh of my flesh; she shall be called Woman because she was taken out of Man."

Therefore a man shall leave his father and his mother and hold fast to his wife, and they shall become one flesh. And the man and his wife were both naked and were not ashamed.

So many things stand out in this passage and you must heed to it if destiny marriage is your desire. God brought Eve to help Adam fulfil God's assignment. God brought someone He had prepared and made fit for destiny.

In Destiny Marriage, the choice is Gods', not yours. If God brought Eve, then she had been in the hand of God – prepared by Him. So allow God to bring someone specifically prepared and equipped for the great destiny, calling and purpose upon your life.

For this to happen you have to sleep like Adam slept. Sleep from your fleshly desires and criteria. You have a great destiny so do not leave marriage to chance. Let God choose and bring you someone that will help you fulfil God's destiny in your life not someone that meets your criteria and appeals to your flesh.

When she helps, you are fulfilled. In God's vision, you find joy and pleasure together. Some effects of a destiny marriage are peace, finance, being a blessing, safety from the world and woes, godly children and etcetera. In God's pleasure, you find pleasure – when your marriage helps you fulfil destiny. In giving God pleasure you find your own pleasure.

Today many men and women seek marriage for their own pleasure – going by their carnal desires, attraction and are lured into satanic bait.

Provers 31 says beauty is charm and deceitful. It never gives what it promises. Seeking their pleasure and fallen into of destruction, missing out on the pleasure that God gives. Many lives and destinies have been destroyed because of this – Isaiah 50: 10-end. Many have failed and are ruined. I don't want you to fail and jeopardize your destiny.

Until Adam slept, Eve was not appreciated. Until Boaz slept, Ruth did not matter. Man sleep from your fleshly perspective so that you will appreciate your God destined wife and help. Amazingly, she is not far from you. God brings her to where you are, you do not go searching. If you are busy with God's vision you do not have the time to search and seek. The only thing man is permitted to seek is God, other things will be added by God including Eve. But when God brings her you have to be spiritual (seeing from the eyes of God) to see her and appreciate her. 1 Corinthians 2:9-16 (*14) ICB. That is why you never access God's mate for you by natural instincts.

If there is any time to be spiritual, it is now so you will not miss it. Boy, you better sleep – mortify fleshly lust and desires and crave fasting and bible study (word up!). It is foolishness to base a choice of a lifetime on things that are temporal like feelings, beauty or age. These are ephemeral and passive.

Ask yourself: Is the man already in the place God is leading me? Is the girl in my scope of God's vision and destiny? Is it God that is bringing this lady to me? Or is it my passions and attractions? Do our destinies match? Are we equally yoked to plough a portion of God's field?

I am not here to tell you not to marry unbelievers that's elementary, but to tell you not to marry any Christian. If you are still on the level of intending to marry someone that is not born again, then your Christianity is questionable and in vain. You are setting yourself up for destruction. You should never marry anyone to change him/her. You can never change an adult that has made up his ways of life. Therefore, as a man or woman of destiny should have made up your ways of life to align with your destiny before committing yourself in to that marriage relationship.

You do not sing in church to glorify God and then sing elsewhere to glorify the devil and the world. Vessels of God are sanctified – set apart. If God is not enough to give you pleasure – El Shaddai, then He is not enough for you for anything else. Choose where you belong, or you are running a great risk; exposing yourself and destiny like Samson.

Remember how God judged King Belshazzar for defiling the Golden Vessels of the Temple of God when he was banqueting with his lords and drinking wine from those consecrated Golden Vessels? In that same hour the fingers of a man's hand appeared and wrote "MENE MENE TEKEL UPHARSIN," pronouncing the doom of the king and his dynasty.

"This is the interpretation of each word. MENE: God has numbered your kingdom, and finished it; 27 TEKEL: You have been weighed in the balances, and found wanting; PERES: Your kingdom has been divided, and given to the Medes and Persians" (Daniel 5:26-28 NKJV).

Samson went to the valley of Sorek, fell in love with Delilah, left his wife of destiny and was destroyed. His going to the valley was the first step to his destruction. Valley symbolizes any place where God is not found. God is found on the mountains – church. Let us go up to the mountain of the Lord. Valley (wild party clubs, casinos, etc.) are shadows of death. All you get and meet there are dead things – dead men and women without God's word, spirit nor vision doing dead things without the life of Christ.

Solomon could not change any of his strange wives, instead, they lured his heart away from God. If you are in that bait, you better remove the hook, off your neck. Have you made a pledge? Quickly take off the hook; Proverbs 6:1-5. Let there be no pity in that deal. A broken engagement is better than a broken marriage. A wrong spouse can lead to your death and take you to hell. Proverbs 5: 1- end ICB.

If the other major decisions in your life are not entirely based on feelings, why base marriage on feelings? God told me that people fail in marriage because they do not take the decision on who to marry seriously. Be intentional and deliberate.

Let's see some examples of good marriages and what they based their choices on. 1 Corinthians 10:11 – the scripture is written for our example so we will be wise and not fail.

Moses' Parents: Exodus 2:1-4 Are from the same family lineage. That is why Moses' great destiny was preserved. I tell you, your choice of marriage affects your children and generations unborn. Choose who has the word of God and is able to teach your kids and pass unto them the word and faith to hide them from destruction and menace in their time.

> *"The Lord says, "I will make an agreement with these people. I promise that my Spirit and my words that I give you will never leave you. They will be with your children and your grandchildren. They will be with you now and forever." Isaiah 59:21 (ICB)*

There must be similarities in families. It must be purpose driven like yours having the same values, priorities, word and spirit. This is why in biblical times; the family tree is considered before marriage which in turn produce godly children. Marriage is more than two people coming together, it is two destiny families coming together uniting forces to affect the next generation.

Abraham and Sarah: Sister and Brother. Marry your sister of the same word and spirit.

Isaac and Rebecca: Not only did Abraham's servant find a wife for Isaac, but Isaac also had a say in that. He took Rebecca to his mother's tent to see if she fits in it. The tent that has kept him thus far, does Rebecca have a place in it?

Parental role and counsel is one of your great asset in the choice of who you marry. No one knows your destiny more than your Holy Spirit-filled parents especially your mother. Like Mary, while my children were in the womb, I knew what God created each one of them to be. And with the same Spirit, I will know who is complementary to their great destinies.

Ruth 3:1 ICB. Naomi said to Ruth I will find a home suitable for you. Not all homes are suitable for my girls because of God's calling on them. Nothing frustrates than unsuitable home. You do not give your pearls to pigs or they will trample it and attack you.

As a destiny child, you do not have any business marrying to a family without a kingdom agenda. My son, listen to the instructions of your mother and the teachings of your father that gave birth to you. What they see sitting down, you will not see even standing on an Iroko tree.

In this context, I am referring to Spirit-led parents that you have proved their counsel over time. Esau's marriage was contrary to the parents' counsel and it took him farther from destiny.

The faith which dwelt first in thy grandmother Lois, and thy mother Eunice; and I am persuaded that in thee also. Ask yourself: the woman I want to marry what spirit and word have been dwelling on her? Do you want to impact that to your children? Make sure the same Spirit of God is on both of you. Only then are you equipped to build a great family and destiny children? Not as one builds another is tearing down.

God is seeking godly seeds He can use to intervene in their generations, as the scripture says.

> *"You were united to your wife by the Lord. In God's wise plan, when you married, the two of you became one person in his sight. And what does he want? Godly children from your union. Therefore, guard your passions! Keep faith with the wife of your youth" (Malachi 2:15 TLB).*

Marry someone that makes your parents' heart glad. The heart connection is important for the transference of destiny. In today's world, there is little or no parental input in the choice of marriage partners. Youths think they know it all and that is why the rate of divorce is high.

> *"Esau, at the age of forty, married a girl named Judith, daughter of Be-eri the Hethite; and he also married Basemath, daughter of Elon the Hethite. But Isaac and Rebekah were bitter about his marrying them" (Genesis 26:34-35 TLB).*

What Samson's parents knew and preserved for his destiny, Delilah knew and destroyed him. There is something your mum/dad know about you – would you allow them to be part of your decision of who she passes on the vision to for your safety and fulfilment?

If you think you know it all, you are setting yourself up for destruction. I tell my daughters that their intelligence doesn't equate the experience of the Holy Spirit's leading; they have come to terms with that.

"Thus saith the LORD, Stand ye in the ways, and see, and ask for the old paths, where is a good way, and walk therein, and ye shall find rest for your souls" (Jeremiah 6:16).

This message shows that old good path that will give you the desired rest for your soul.

I love you so much and it is my desire that you succeed and be fulfilled. Carrying on the PDF legacy. The devil has lost it forever in your life. Amen.

In summary, marriage is not only intended to fulfil sensual appeal but to fulfil destinies. Marry for kingdom sake and you will be happy and fulfilled. Those that lose their lives, shall find it. Those that try to keep it shall lose it.

Go To Your Parents/Mum: Ask them what God told them about you. Then ask them what woman or man they think fits in for your life. If you have one already, ask them their genuine opinion of the relationship.

God gave me a word for someone reading this. In Genesis 24:67 Isaac took Rebecca to his mum's tent and was comforted. Until the person you choose as a wife fits your mum's tent – your mum's spiritual abode, prayer life, word, walk of faith – you will never be comforted nor fulfilled. If your mum is still alive and dwells in a tent of prayer and faith, involve her in your choice.

> *"And Isaac brought Rebekah into his mother's tent, and she became his wife. He loved her very much, and she was a special comfort to him after the loss of his mother" (Genesis 24:67 TLB).*

It is your mum's tent that preserves you and makes your life comfortable and secured amidst the devil's wiles and assaults. You still need a tent even as a man but no longer your mum's. So make sure you will have the right tent.

Always realize that you have come this far because of your mum's tent. If you must go further, you need a tent. Before you leave and cleave to her, make sure she has a reliable tent of faith and prayer. Many men are open to attacks because there is no spiritual tent of covering.

When someone measures up to your mum's tent or can grow into it you will find love and comfort in that marriage. This is critical to the success of that union.

Note: Mum will die someday, and you will need a tent. Marry someone spiritual to provide that coverage for you and your kids.

When you fall in love blindly before marriage, you have already started falling – possibly, never to rise again. You are to grow in love for lasting destiny marriage.

Lastly, if you marry for broad chest and 6 inches then that broad chest will be your punching board. What do I mean? Do not be controlled by feelings. Open your eyes and choose based on godly virtues and this will automatically stimulate genuine love. The love for mum is the most genuine love in a man's heart so if you find someone that fits her tent that same genuine love will develop, and it will stand the test of time.

I tell you; marriages have challenges and you need genuine love to weather through them. Isaac, despite the challenges, had a hitch-free marriage. Who says you cannot have a hitch-free marriage?

Someone reading this book has a destiny like that of Isaac but be wise in your choice of marriage. I tell you, any girl you marry based on emotions, shortly after the wedding the love will fizzle away. And ladies, make sure the mum of the potential man has a tent (faith walk) or the man will be confused. It will be like putting a square pen in a round hole.

God bless you as you make wise choice and carry on the PDF legacy to the coming generations.